In Defence of Democracy

In Defence of Democracy

Roslyn Fuller

polity

First published in 2019 by Polity Press

Polity Press
65 Bridge Street
Cambridge CB2 1UR, UK

Polity Press
101 Station Landing
Suite 300
Medford, MA 02155, USA

ISBN-13: 978-1-5095-3312-1
ISBN-13: 978-1-5095-3313-8 (pb)

A catalogue record for this book is available from the British Library.

Library of Congress Cataloging-in-Publication Data

Names: Fuller, Roslyn, author.
Title: In defence of democracy / Roslyn Fuller.
Other titles: In defense of democracy
Description: Cambridge, UK ; Medford, MA : Polity, [2019] | Includes
  bibliographical references and index.
Identifiers: LCCN 2019004023 (print) | LCCN 2019016699 (ebook) | ISBN
  9781509533152 (Epub) | ISBN 9781509533121 (hardback) | ISBN 9781509533138
  (pbk.)
Subjects: LCSH: Democracy--Philosophy.
Classification: LCC JC423 (ebook) | LCC JC423 .F895 2019 (print) | DDC
  321.8--dc23
LC record available at https://lccn.loc.gov/2019004023

Typeset in 11 on 14 pt Sabon by
Servis Filmsetting Ltd, Stockport, Cheshire
Printed and bound in Great Britain by TJ International Limited

For further information on Polity, visit our website: politybooks.com

Contents

Introduction: Why This? Why Me? Why Now?   1

Part I   The Terrible Truth: People Aren't All
           That Stupid or Evil   11

Objection One: Democracy Can't Work Because
    People Are Too Racist and Sexist   12
Objection Two: People Are Too Stupid for
    Democracy   28
Objection Three: There's No Point to Democracy
    Because People Don't Know What Is Good for
    Them Anyway   36
Objection Four: People Are Just Too Crazy
    for Democracy to Work   53
To Conclude   68

Part II   Fixing Politics the Anti-Democrat Way   75

Section 1 Assorted Libertarian, Authoritarian and
           Explicitly Elitist Solutions   75
    Rule by the 'knowledgeable' (Jason Brennan)   75
    Rule by the deep state (Bryan Caplan)   80

Contents

Rule by the market (Ilya Somin)   83

Long live the party! (Jonathan Rauch and
    Benjamin Wittes)   87

Rule of the superior (Daniel Bell)   94

Section 2 Sortition: The False Democrats   102

Participation   107

Representation and legitimacy   122

Politics is conflict mediation   127

Corruption   130

Conclusions on sortition   136

Conclusions to Part II   138

**Part III A World You Might Want to Actually
Live In (Fuller Democracy)**   **141**

Five Principles for Transformational (but
    Responsible) People Power   147

1 Shift to online and en masse   147

2 Pay-for-participation   165

3 Focused, outcome-oriented deliberation
    (information, *isegoria* and conflict resolution)   172

4 Precarious, informal leadership (but
    leadership all the same)   189

5 Sortition in its proper place   196

Why It's Worth It   207

1 People want democracy   207

2 Fuller democracy solves a lot of anti-
    democrat objections to democracy   210

3 Writing a new social contract   214

**Final Words: Buckle-up Buttercup: The Future
Is Going to be Interesting**   **217**

Notes   223

Index   255

Introduction: Why This? Why Me? Why Now?

When I first started writing about democracy in 2006, I did not feel the need to defend the *idea* of self-government. After all, back in those halcyon days, people who started a conversation on why there shouldn't be democracy often quickly moved on to why Hitler wasn't *totally* wrong, with occasional asides on the merits of tin foil hats. To be *against* democracy, *against* majority rule, *against* political equality *as concepts* was considered to be vaguely treasonous and definitely pretty fringe.

Unfortunately, only a dozen years later, things have changed dramatically.

There are plenty of people willing to attack the idea of democracy today, and they are agreed on what the problem is: the 'demos' bit, that is 'the people' – specifically anyone who doesn't belong to what they define as the class of 'superior',[1] 'respectable elite'[2] or 'knowledgeable'[3] persons.

This latest wave of anti-democrats is of a decidedly new and peculiar stripe. Unlike so many of their predecessors, they don't sport swastika tattoos or dispose over small but varied arsenals of pilfered Apocalypse-ready army materiel. Instead, you'll find twenty-first-century anti-democrats lounging in professorial chairs, clinking glasses at intellectual soirées and delivering their opinions on the faults of the masses straight into camera on prime time. Some of these new anti-democrats are libertarians, others are liberals, still others technocratic centrists, but they all have something in common: they oppose the idea of majority rule; they reject the doctrine of human equality; they deny the inherent value of one-person, one-vote. Philosophers now openly argue that some people don't deserve a voice in politics;[4] professors preach that it is permissible to ignore the popular will because people don't *actually* want the things they say they want;[5] newspaper editors float the idea that maybe it's time to just give up on the whole democracy thing.

Like medieval inquisitors, these new anti-democrats claim to have always known the horrible 'truth' about humanity – that we are all just too stupid and evil for politics – they were just waiting for proof so that they could swing into action.

With Britain's vote in favour of leaving the European Union in June 2016 (the so-called 'Brexit' referendum) and the election of President Donald Trump in the United States in November of the same year, they're sure that they've finally got it. At last, the people have been caught red-handed exercising their virulent racism, sexism and general stupidity at the ballot box, bringing poor government upon us all. Since 'the people' were at the base of these two 'wrong' votes, the obvious answer is to cut them out of politics and allow society to be governed by an 'enlightened minority' that would never have voted for either Trump or Brexit.

This version of events, which casts majority rule as an illegitimate *evil* and a self-proclaimed enlightened minority as a noble *good*, has, despite its arrogant and fanatic overtones, been persistently put across by the political left, right and centre over the past few years with an insistence as pervasive as it is aggressive. In an October 2016 article published in the *Guardian*, philosopher Julian Baggini described trusting the majority 'to reach fair and wise decisions' as 'borderline insane', before telling us that 'Plato and Aristotle get a bad rap these days for their rejection of democracy. But the substance of their objections were spot-on.'[6] According to the *Spiegel Online*, Brexit is nothing less than an 'abuse' of 'direct democracy' that shows that '[i]n our complex 21st century world, we have no choice but to delegate authority for most decision-making to our elected representatives'.[7] British human rights lawyer Geoffrey Robertson urged MPs to overturn the Brexit vote because '[d]emocracy has never meant the tyranny of the simple majority',[8] while the UK *Independent* ran articles arguing that some things are just 'too important to be decided by the people'[9] and accusing British MPs of hiding 'behind the vapid UKIP mantra – the so-called will of the people'.[10] According to Mai'a K. Davis Cross, Professor of Political Science at Northeastern University in Boston, there is 'Nothing Democratic About Brexit'.[11] Gerard Delanty, Professor of Sociology at the University of Sussex, agreed in his post, 'Brexit and the Great Pretence of Democracy' that 'the notion that 50 per cent plus one is an acceptable threshold is a fiction',[12] while in *Foreign Policy* James Traub let us know that it is 'Time for the Elites to Rise Up Against the Ignorant Masses'.[13] Belgian author David van Reybrouck called the Brexit referendum a 'primitive procedure' and a 'blunt axe wielded by disenchanted and poorly informed citizens',[14] while former *Independent* journalist Richard Askwith warned readers that they were about to be overrun by the 'tyranny of the mob'.[15] Simon Wren-Lewis, Professor of Economics at Oxford, proclaimed: 'You may say that Leave Voters will lose their faith in the democratic system if Brexit doesn't happen, but the same is surely true of Republican voters if Obamacare is not repealed. That is hardly a reason to do it.'[16] In 'More Professionalism, Less Populism: How Voting Makes Us Stupid and What to Do About It',[17] Brookings Fellows Jonathan Rauch and Benjamin Wittes argued for less participation by the average person and more 'intermediation' by institutions built from a political class empowered to do no less than engage in corrupt practices for everyone's sake. Kenneth Rogoff, former Chief Economist of the IMF and a professor at Harvard, declared that simple majority rule is 'a formula for chaos' and this 'isn't democracy',[18] while Daniel W. Drezner at Tufts University proclaimed that '*Of course*, there can be too much democracy'.[19] Last, but not least, in their much quoted book *Democracy for Realists*,[20] Professors Christopher Achen and Larry Bartels promulgated research that purported to show that people are so incapable of expressing their own best interests at the ballot box that elections are won and lost on everything from shark attacks to the weather; an interview with the authors ran on *Vox* under the headline 'The Problem with Democracy is Voters'.[21]

While these writers by and large consider themselves to be liberal progressives, or at least centrist technocrats, whose sole noble aim consists of rescuing the ignorant from themselves, when it comes to democracy they're singing off the same hymn sheet as their decidedly more conservative and libertarian brethren. According to Jason Brennan, Georgetown University philosopher and author of *Against Democracy*, the stupid and ignorant should simply be disenfranchised, a state of affairs he terms 'epistocracy' or 'rule by the knowledgeable'. *Against Democracy* was reviewed in *The New Yorker*[22] and *The Washington Post*,[23] and Brennan's genius concept of simply depriving people of their right to vote was deemed so worthy of discussion that numerous papers published his op-eds[24] elaborating on his view that: 'In an epistocracy, not everyone has the same voting power. But what's so wrong with that?'[25] Brennan is buttressed by fellow academics and Cato Institute scholars Ilya Somin and Bryan Caplan, whose numerous op-eds[26] and books, such as *Democracy and Political Ignorance*[27] and the *Myth of the Rational Voter*,[28] repeatedly excoriate the 'ignorance' of any voters who happen to disagree with their views on labour regulation and free trade. Canadian academic Daniel Bell provides a snobbier twist on the same theme in his book *The China Model: Political Meritocracy and the Limits of Democracy*, arguing for rule by an unelected virtuous 'superior' elite.

Right-wing journalists haven't just been generous in granting column inches and interviews to these authors, either; they've been more than willing to chime in against wayward voters themselves. According to James Kirchick, writing in the *Los Angeles Times*, the 2017 British election in which Jeremy Corbyn's Labour Party surged in the polls is 'a Reminder of the Perils of Too Much Democracy', because '"the people" – that expression beloved of Third World tyrants and increasingly adopted by leaders in advanced industrial democracies – got their say'. Kirchick went on to claim: 'Amidst the global populist insurgency, our duly elected representatives should depend more upon their own judgment and worry less about the uninformed opinion of the masses.'[29] In *New York Magazine*, Andrew Sullivan confidently informed the world that 'Democracies End When They Are Too Democratic';[30] at *Bloomberg*, Justin Fox opined that 'Voters are Making a Mess of Democracy';[31] and in the *New York Times*, Bret Stephens claimed that 'the people' are responsible for 'anti-Semitism masquerading as anti-Zionism; anti-Americanism masquerading as pacifism; fellow-traveling with dictators and terrorists masquerading as sympathy for the wretched of the earth', which evils apparently manifest themselves in voting for long-time MP and current British Labour Party leader Jeremy Corbyn.[32]

It's endless, it's alarming (and purposely alarmist) and it's bullshit. In fact, it is all so ridiculous and shoddily researched that were these books and articles to be published at all, it should have been in the entertainment section. 'E for effort', my mother often says when confronted with a piece of particular stupidity, but this doesn't even rate that. F for failure, F for fraud, and F for trying to fuck you over.

And it is no coincidence at all that this is coming out of the woodwork now.

The anti-democratic movement isn't really, when it gets down to it, about Trump or Brexit. It's about something else entirely, something much bigger.

You see, agreeing to the *theoretical principle* of political equality is a different ball of wax entirely than agreeing to the *reality* of it. But up until now an agreement in *principle* was all that was required of anyone who wanted to label themselves a democrat.

This is because democracy has traditionally been a fairly passive activity, involving nothing more impactful than casting a ballot for one of a tiny number of candidates every few years. For practical reasons only very small numbers of people could be directly involved in politics on a daily basis and for that reason it has been the nature of the beast that in our democracy to date there has been a split between the *ideology* of equal participation and the *practical reality* of elites running the show: political elites drafted and voted on laws; media elites decided which stories to publish; financial elites determined which candidates and parties to back. *Thinking, speaking* and *acting* publicly were activities that the average person had virtually no share in. The occasional mass mobilization surfaced when things were really tough, but such movements were rare and difficult to get off the ground, because it was impossible even to know what millions of individuals thought or wanted at any given time, much less effectively channel that into action or any kind of government.

But now it is impossible *not* to know.

Technology finally managed to do what it promised to do for so long – disrupt things – and it did so by sending the cost of political participation through the floor. *Thinking, speaking* and *acting* publicly, and therefore politically, has within a few short years become as cheap as it is easy. Suddenly, anyone and everyone can engage in political action on their own at any time. People who had for decades become comfortable saying that they supported ordinary citizens holding power as an ideal, but that it sadly just wasn't possible, have woken up to a world where it *is* possible. And they don't seem to like it quite as much as they claimed they would.

Indeed, the theoretical understanding that people held power in our democracies, but that this rather conveniently manifested itself in passively receiving information and instructions from 'the respectable elite', suddenly clashes very, very hard with a real-world set of circumstances in which the traditional middlemen of politics – politicians, journalists, academics – are no longer strictly speaking necessary for the system to operate. You don't need a reporter to tell you what is going on in India or China when you can get on Facebook and ask someone who lives there; you don't always need to 'ask an expert' when you can access more information than you will ever be able to digest on Wikipedia and YouTube; and if you want to know what people think about current affairs, you need look no farther than the comments section of any major news website. From a 'value-added' point of view, the traditional power-broking jobs are taking a nosedive, as rather than facilitating participation, as they previously (to some extent) had done, they have become a bottleneck for something that could happen more efficiently without them.

Just as we can book our own flight tickets and manage our stock portfolios online, we no longer technically need anyone to guess 'what the people want' or tell us 'what everyone thinks', because it is possible to acquire that information directly.

Thus, the elites who traditionally exercised the political functions of speaking, thinking and acting publicly on behalf of everyone else are rapidly becoming surplus to requirements. If democracy continues to evolve with advances in technology, it will naturally become more participatory and direct, because not only is it now possible for people to communicate easily on a peer-to-peer basis and thus to coordinate political action without involving middlemen, it is already foreseeable that this trend will only continue into the future. If elites want to prevent that from happening – and many of them do consciously or unconsciously want just that – they have no choice but to attack the idea of democracy and convince us (the people) that we cannot trust each other and *need* the elites – not to fulfil traditional democratic functions (like providing information or a best-guess at the popular will) that would otherwise go unmet, but to save us from ourselves.

In other words, they are attempting to change their job description, because, like a courtier around Louis XVI, they have begun to have a vague sense of foreboding that if the *ancien régime* goes down they are going with it. In this changed world, the only hope for anti-democrats to maintain their prestige and power is to clamp down and exclude the ungrateful masses even further from political life than they have been in the past.

And they are hard at work on doing just that, which is why I think this book is so necessary.

In the following pages I'm going to examine some of the most celebrated arguments and research purporting to show that the problem with democracy is the people; that they are stupid, that they are racist, that they are incapable of assessing their own welfare; that we must give up on political equality for our own good; that disagreement is the same as treason; that the worthy must be separated from the unworthy; that submitting to control is the only way to be safe.

While, as I will show, these claims are every bit as crazy as they appear to be on the surface, anti-democrats have already made progress in putting them into action and attempting to restrict the principle of one-person, one-vote.

Their proposed solutions to cure democracy of its 'people problem' – and we will go into these in some detail – range from the apparently brilliantly simple ('don't let them vote') to the somewhat more subtly complex ('select people at random and subject them to expert lectures until they agree to do the right thing'). Anti-democrats around the world have already established well-funded institutions and organizations to implement these strategies and bring about their goal of sanitizing democracy from the 'demos'. And the very fact that anti-democrats have managed to get this far means that now we – the masses, as it were – are at a crossroads, too.

We *don't* actually have to sit by and watch our civilization dissolve into a dystopian hellscape of warring factions or rigid, hierarchical control. We have the means to make things better – to make a more participatory and inclusive democracy than any of us has ever known – and we should grasp those possibilities with both hands.

Democracy isn't getting worse – it's getting better.

Some people just don't want democracy.

Part I

The Terrible Truth: People Aren't All That Stupid or Evil

The first objective in the anti-democrat strategy is to create the idea that there are insurmountable 'problems' that make it impossible for one-person, one-vote majority rule to work. Unto itself, it is a fairly inchoate argument – the main point isn't really to lead to any specific conclusions (that comes later), but merely to firmly anchor the idea that the biggest single problem with politics as we know it is ... people. So if things aren't 100 per cent satisfactory, then that is where the blame clearly lies. People, as a generality, just aren't *good enough* for democracy to work. In fact, people are nothing less than stupid and evil.

Anti-democratic writers engage in a kind of Tet Offensive on the human psyche to try to drive home this point – articles decrying the depraved state of the average human and its fatal effect on politics can be found in virtually every newspaper virtually every day.

This onslaught, however, is based on half-truths, strange flights of fancy, leaps in logic that don't hold up under the slightest scrutiny and point-blank factually inaccurate statements. Just a few minutes of scrutiny are enough to show that even the anti-democrats' strongest and most coherent points on human fallibility make about as much sense as a bad piece of Dadaist poetry; that there really is nothing to the claim that 'the people' are dangerous, that their will is bad for humankind and that they need to be controlled by the benevolent few for everyone's sake.

Let's take a closer look.

Objection One: Democracy Can't Work Because People Are Too Racist and Sexist

That's right: one-person, one-vote democracy can't work because people are racist and sexist. This is a specialized form of the more general 'people are crazy' argument that we'll look at later on, but with an ugly twist. The crux of this thesis is that many people don't *really* want the policies or politicians they vote for, but rather that they are led to vote a certain way due to their uncontrollable tendencies to racism and sexism which override all reason. Since these votes aren't 'real' but merely the by-products of irrational and evil tendencies, it would only be right to discount them. Anti-democrats are a little vague on exactly how this would be achieved, but they are fairly clear on the point that political participation should not necessarily be a universal right, but rather something accorded only to people who possess a certain minimum level of 'virtue'.

To give a flavour of how this sentiment is propagated: on 17 February 2018, science writer Ben Goldacre retweeted a Venn diagram in which circles labelled 'racists' and 'idiots' overlapped to form a category identified as 'racist idiots', adding the caption: 'Brexit voters get tremendously upset when you say they are racists and idiots. I think they misunderstand the criticism. This Venn diagram communicates the issue very clearly. I hope it can bring some healing.'[1]

Joining this general sentiment in his exhortation to the elite to rise up against the ignorant masses, *Foreign Policy* columnist James Traub speaks of Leave and Trump voters as an 'angry, nationalist rank and file' and as 'people whose familiar world is vanishing beneath a welter of foreign tongues and multicultural celebrations'.[2] Others argue that 'psychological predictors of xenophobia were strongly linked with voting to leave the EU',[3] while the leader of the British pro-Remain Liberal Democrat party stated that Leave voters longed for 'a time when faces were white and the map was coloured imperial pink'.[4] In America, where, it appears, the wonders of the Venn diagram haven't been discovered, arguments rage between pundits as to whether Trump voters are idiots[5] or racists[6] (but apparently not both), while Hillary Clinton's difficulty in securing the Democratic Party nomination as well as her ultimate defeat in the 2016 presidential election is repeatedly blamed on sexism, not least by Clinton herself.[7]

So, the question is: are we there?

Have racism and sexism skyrocketed in the UK and the USA in past years to the point that our only hope lies in forgetting democracy as we know it, capping the political rights of the unworthy (albeit in some ill-defined way) and throwing ourselves on the mercies of the blessed elite to ensure that the morally 'right' decisions are always taken? Have things deteriorated to the point where we need to predetermine which votes are good and which votes are not? Is it time we accepted that some people just don't *deserve* to participate in the same way as others?

Let's start with the 2016 Democratic Party presidential primary in the USA.

The argument here is that Hillary Clinton's lack of popularity with traditional Democratic voters was not related to her policies or political record, but rather to racism and sexism on the part of the voters themselves. It is this irrational racism and sexism that 'distorts' electoral outcomes from the 'true' considered will of the people, and provokes the need for anti-democrats to find 'innovative' ways to improve democracy by reducing the impact of those votes. In pursuit of this argument, anti-democrats frequently label supporters of Bernie Sanders, Clinton's main rival in the 2016 Democratic primary, 'Bernie Bros' – white men who supported Bernie over Hillary out of sexist and racist motives. In their widely read book *Democracy for Realists*, political science professors Christopher Achen and Larry Bartels note that Bernie Sanders polled eleven points worse among women than among men and eighteen points worse among non-whites than among whites. Thus, they conclude that voters did not actually espouse Sanders's left-wing policies, but rather that the Jewish septuagenarian with a forty-year track record as an Independent politician was merely 'a convenient vehicle for anti-Clinton sentiment … especially [among] white men'.[8]

That's right – Bernie supporters *didn't* want universal healthcare, affordable tuition fees or a somewhat less warmongering foreign policy. They just *said* all that to rationalize their true motives of being racist and sexist 'disaffected white men' who wanted to follow a politician from 'lily white Vermont' for deeper identitarian reasons.[9]

It's quite the claim.

Maybe if people don't vote for any *actual reasons*, but merely to express their group identity, one-person, one-vote democracy *doesn't* make sense.

But ... the data adds up to a very different picture.

While Clinton *did* win more female votes during the primaries, as those who favour the sexism narrative for her flagging popularity like to point out, what they're a little less keen on is the fact that Bernie Sanders consistently polled higher among young women than Clinton did, about ... *500–600 per cent higher.*

To say that is off the charts doesn't even begin to cover it. In fact, during the primaries, the difference in voting preferences between the youngest and oldest female cohorts was greater than the difference between male and female voting preferences.

At the Iowa primary, 84 per cent of under 30s *and 86 per cent of women* under 30 indicated a preference for Sanders, with only 14 per cent in favour of Clinton,[10] while in New Hampshire, Sanders took 82 per cent of votes from women under 30.[11] Just a month before he formally ended his campaign, Sanders was still polling 37 percentage points ahead of Clinton with women aged 18–29.[12]

And he wasn't just more popular with young women, either. In an analysis of twenty-five state primaries, Sanders won under-30s black support by 52 per cent compared to Clinton's 47 per cent. In another survey, black millennials reported voting for Sanders over Clinton by 44 per cent to 32 per cent.[13]

So Achen and Bartels aren't lying when they say

that Clinton won both the black and female vote in the Democratic primaries, but explaining this as a factor of racism and sexism is only possible by concealing the whole truth – that Clinton did not win these demographics across the board, but rather through her overwhelming popularity with the oldest cohorts, who often outnumbered younger voters. For example, in the aforementioned twenty-five-state survey, Clinton won over-60s black votes by 89 per cent compared to 9 per cent for Sanders; that helped because over-60s black voters outnumbered under-30s black voters by more than 2:1.[14]

The pattern held true for other groups as well. An *LA Times*/USC survey put support among Latinos under 50 for Bernie at 58 per cent versus Hillary at 31 per cent, while among Latinos over-50 support for Sanders was at 16 per cent versus 69 per cent for Clinton.[15] Young Asian Americans were also apparently more drawn to Sanders, with 75 per cent of 18–34-year-olds viewing him favourably, compared to 55 per cent for Clinton.[16]

When 18–30-year-olds were asked who they wanted to win the Democratic nomination in June 2016 (just weeks before the Democratic convention), the breakdown according to race was as follows:

- African Americans: Sanders 53 per cent, Clinton 39 per cent;
- Asian Americans: Sanders 69 per cent, Clinton 21 per cent;
- Latino/as: Sanders 71 per cent, Clinton 24 per cent;
- non-Hispanic whites: Sanders 62 per cent, Clinton 32 per cent.[17]

According to these figures, young Asian Americans and Latinos liked Sanders even more than their Caucasian counterparts did.

If Bernie Bros were so racist and sexist, why were so many of them female and non-white?

Perhaps because these young voters weren't unthinking automatons motivated by an identitarian kinship with an old white man, but were in fact deeply concerned about important issues such as wages and education, which they felt were not being adequately addressed by Clinton.[18] In any event, the numbers clearly show that the Great Divider of the 2016 Democratic Party contest was not race or sex – it was age.

Rather than negotiate with younger voters, Clinton's campaign attempted to coerce them into changing their allegiances by implying that they 'owed' their vote to Clinton. Feminist icon and Clinton-supporter Gloria Steinem, for example, claimed that young female Sanders supporters were not motivated by their own political convictions but by the prospect of meeting boys at rallies, while former Secretary of State Madeleine Albright told them they were going to hell for failing to support another woman.[19]

These heavy-handed and insultingly patronizing tactics do not appear to have endeared Clinton to younger voters and her lack of popularity continued throughout her presidential campaign against Donald Trump. In particular, polls indicated that Clinton was less popular among young people of colour than Obama had been (despite having the obvious advantage that her opponent was Donald Trump, a candidate whose platform included building a border wall with Mexico).[20] Compared to the previous election, young black turn-out was lower,[21] while many young voters opted for third-party candidates.[22] Attributing Trump's victory to resurgent discrimination overlooks both that Clinton failed to motivate key sectors of her own base, for the rather obvious reason that, unlike Bernie, she didn't offer policy that served their interests, and that Trump *still lost* the popular vote by a significant margin. Rather than Trump's campaign presenting a kind of reinvigorated goosestep to victory, the 2016 presidential campaign was lacklustre, with considerable voter apathy on both sides. Indeed, it is noteworthy that in this alleged existential battle between good and evil, turn-out barely topped 60 per cent.[23]

As if that weren't enough, even among those who voted for Trump, racism and sexism are hard to discern as primary motivating factors.

During a stay in Indiana a year after Trump took office, *Guardian* reporter Gary Younge interviewed a number of residents who not only voted for Trump, but continued to be satisfied with his activities in office. Despite their continued political support, nearly everyone Younge spoke to disapproved of Trump's bombastic and, at times, offensive persona. One voter stated that '[He is] a 70-year-old white man. He's been supported in bigotry his entire life. He's been validated his entire life. And people wonder why he acts like this', before referring to him as 'like your drunk uncle at a party'. Another referred to Trump's tweets as 'word-vomit' that made them 'cringe'. However, his voters still felt that Trump was a necessary evil. One of them cited the need for disruption in politics ('disruption's never easy. But it is important') while another said that the most important thing was to get things done, explicitly stating: 'I would take an arsehole doctor who was going to fix me over a nice guy who wouldn't. The nice guy doesn't always get things done.'[24]

This feedback squares with a Bloomberg report two months before the election (sixteen months before Younge journeyed to Indiana). Among likely voters without a college degree, Trump's most positive points were seen as: 'changing Washington, knowing what it takes to create jobs, and "sharing my views on dealing with undocumented immigrants"' while his *number one* negative point was: 'his verbal treatment of women, including calling them names'. Of all non-college educated likely voters, 56 per cent said that they were 'bothered a lot' by this and it was closely followed by the Trump University lawsuit, Trump's tax plan and also, notably, white supremacist support for Trump.[25] In other words, Trump's sexist language and the fact that he was endorsed by white supremacists were identified as major obstacles by 'uneducated' voters.

Trump, it would appear, did not get elected *because* he deeply appealed to the lurking bigots around – he got elected *despite* the fact that many people found these aspects off-putting. In exit polls, fewer than 20 per cent of voters said they strongly favoured him. Take a moment to reflect that exit polls happen *right after* someone casts a ballot, and it becomes apparent that voters were far from carried away by any kind of perceived group loyalty, but were rather engaged in what was in their view an uninspiring but necessary task. Indeed, 11 per cent of voters who said Trump's treatment of women bothered them a lot *still* voted for him, while 73 per cent of those who said it bothered them somewhat did.

But among voters who rated a candidate's ability to bring change as the most important quality, 82 per cent voted for Trump.[26]

Bernie voters wanted change; Trump voters wanted change. Indeed, President Obama rocketed to the White House on a particularly captivating platform of change. The key motivations of voters are really quite clear and have been stable for some time. If anything, the desire for change *transcended* the ethnic profile of candidates; Obama, Trump and Bernie all come from different ethnic backgrounds – their common denominator was not their identity, but rather their promise of change.

So while racism and sexism are undoubtedly issues in American society, anti-democrats fall far short of demonstrating that American voters unthinkingly cast votes based on identity rather than policy and that these votes should thus somehow be invalidated.

The lack of substance, however, hasn't stopped anti-democrats from using the racism and sexism argument as a kind of multipurpose explanation for all that confounds them.

In particular, many insist on viewing racism as practically the sole factor in Britain's vote to leave the European Union.

After all, UK Independence Party (UKIP) leader and prominent Leave campaigner Nigel Farage's many media appearances standing in front of posters with everything up to and including a depiction of escalators apparently meant to deliver the ravening hordes over 'The Wall' from Game of Thrones[27] and into rural Britain must have had *some* effect. Furthermore, the Syrian refugee crisis was ongoing for some time prior to the referendum and campaigners sometimes drew a link between EU membership and obligations to take in refugees,* while others described refugees with contempt. In 2015, a year before the referendum, *Sun* columnist Katie Hopkins even referred to refugees as 'vermin', a 'virus' and 'cockroaches', and suggested the military be deployed to shoot them.[28]

However, whether one can translate each and every Leave vote into full-fledged support for the most extravagant statements of prominent Leave supporters, as anti-democrats frequently attempt to do, is highly questionable.

While Katie Hopkins eventually lost her media platforms, she still frequently tweets explicitly racist comments to her 844,000 Twitter followers. For example, on 18 March 2018, she tweeted:

* Another poster featuring a line of Middle Eastern refugees under the slogan 'Breaking point' was heavily criticized; see, e.g., Oliver Wright, 'EU referendum: Nigel Farage's anti-migrant poster like 1930s fascist propaganda says George Osborne', *UK Independent* (19 June 2016), https://www.independent.co.uk/news/uk/politics/eu-referendum-poster-nigel-farage-polls-michael-gove-a7089946.html.

(The tweet refers to a child abuse ring predominately operated by British Asian men that had been exposed in Telford).

Fascinatingly, a recurring trend, *even among people who publicly expressed general support for Hopkins*, was protest at her use of the caveat 'white'. It thus seems reasonable to conclude that at least some of Hopkins's supporters are lagging behind her in the racism department. And that is among people who have, for reasons best known to themselves, clicked the 'follow' button on Katie Hopkins's profile. Out in the wider world, a change.org petition to prevent Hopkins from being removed from LBC radio after tweeting about a 'final solution' in the aftermath of the Manchester bombing in May 2017 received only 11,929 signatures after ten months,[29] whereas a petition on the same platform to have her removed from the *Sun* newspaper garnered 310,000 signatures, and one that proposed exchanging Hopkins for 50,000 Syrian refugees got 20,000 signatures in just forty-eight hours. In other words, a satirical petition to exchange Hopkins for refugees got nearly twice as many votes in less than 1 per cent of the time as one to prevent her being removed from her radio show.

As this highlights, Hopkins, like many people who work in media, is a largely self-appointed leader – a grassroots mandate cannot necessarily be inferred. When she stood as an Independent candidate in the 2009 European election, despite being relatively well known as a reality show contestant, she received just 0.6 per cent of the vote in her electoral district, an area that largely voted Leave in the 2016 Brexit referendum. In that same year (2009), UKIP received 30 per cent of the vote share in the area, while the overtly racist

British National Party received 3.9 per cent. Thus, it would seem that UKIP and its point-based immigration policy are about as far-right as any significant number of people have shown themselves willing to go, even when explicitly presented with more racist voting possibilities. While people like Hopkins are hired for their ability to consistently outrage others and generate controversy – and they certainly succeed – it is reckless to conclude from that that their every utterance enjoys popular backing, even among people who may share other views – like voting Leave – with them.

Indeed, an ICM poll found that 56 per cent of British people 'support a controlled migration system where immigrants contribute to society', with only 36 per cent point blank wanting to reduce the number of immigrants.[30] A separate multinational IPSOS MORI poll found that in comparison to other European countries, Brits had unusually positive attitudes towards immigration,[31] and had become significantly *more* positive between 2011 and 2017.[32] In particular, the study found that attitudes towards immigration had *softened* since the Brexit referendum.[33]

As all of this indicates, the exact link between a Leave vote, views on immigration and racism is hard to quantify. After all, membership in the European Union, the actual issue at stake in the Brexit vote, privileges predominately white European immigrants, while immigrants from other, predominantly non-white nations face far greater hurdles to entering the UK.[34] If points-based immigration were applied to all entrants, it would almost certainly *benefit* highly qualified individuals from predominately non-white nations. Perhaps because of this, in the run-up to the referendum up to one-third of ethnic minority voters said that they intended to vote Leave.[35]

That racism exists and can motivate how someone casts their vote is not in doubt. Indeed, racism and sexism probably did play *some* role in the Brexit vote and in Trump's election (at least the overt 'keep them out racism' as opposed to the 'bring them in and let them mind my kids for cheap while I condescend to them' variety). But that either outcome was an example of racism suddenly run riot in its most virulent forms – forms so extreme as to call into question the very legitimacy of the referendum/election, not to mention the principle of majority rule itself – doesn't stack up.

Especially when we take a little trip down memory lane.

It turns out that back in the days of elite rule, the track record on minorities was, shall we say, less than amazing.

You may recall, for example, colonialism, that interesting adventure wherein Europeans – most prominent among them the British – sailed around the world, forcibly changing other people's religion, customs and ways of dress, while taking their best land, and making them work very, very hard in menial positions. When the Mau Mau of Kenya revolted *in 1952* after being driven off their land by British settlers, the Empire responded by putting them in concentration camps, torturing, executing and in some cases even castrating them. It took more than fifty years for their case for compensation to come to court.[36] Then there was Belgian King Leopold, who acquired the Congo Free State as his personal property and – in what could definitely be termed a myopic strategy – got his minions to go around killing people who didn't work hard enough. Or Iberian conquistadors, who funnelled a river of gold and silver back to Europe from South America while initiating the Atlantic slave trade that was to predominate for hundreds of years. The list goes on. Suffice it to say that general trends of racism and sexism continued, though in gradually reduced form, through the practice of forcibly removing indigenous children from their homes to assimilate them, which prevailed in the US, Canada and Australia until the 1960s,* while, in many Western countries, women had to leave a public job when they married up until the 1970s, a time that coincides with them being allowed to vote in federal elections in Switzerland. 'The weaker sex' and their various imaginary shortcomings were favourite topics of conversation, and are often casually referred to in many older books and films. Mansplaining, hepeating and sexual harassment were all definitely 'things' before either Trump, Brexit or the Internet appeared on the scene.

The existence of the KKK, founded in 1865 and boasting a peak membership of more than four million in the 1920s (compared to a few thousand today);[37] segregation; the fact that, prior to Obama, every single President of the United States was both male and white; the 1964 British election in which Conservative MP Peter Griffiths campaigned *successfully* on the alleged slogan, 'If you want a n***** for a neighbour, vote Liberal or Labour';† the signs on businesses common in both

---

* The last Canadian residential school closed in the mid-1990s.

† Griffiths himself claimed to have never used the slogan and that the Labour Party had invented it to discredit him ('Peter Griffiths – Obituary', *Telegraph* (27 November 2013)), although he also allegedly told a reporter that he 'would not condemn any man who used such a slogan'; see Stuart

the UK and the USA reading 'No Blacks. No Irish. No Dogs';[38] not to mention Enoch Powell's 'rivers of blood' speech in which he, at the time UK Shadow Minister for Defence, took up the cause of a 'poor woman' who was impoverishing herself through her apparently noble unwillingness to rent to non-whites* might have sufficed to tip off the casual observer that there might be a few racism and sexism problems around.

Go back even further to the pre-Enlightenment days, when elite rule was the norm and you'll find that the threshold on killing, torturing and expropriating people of different races and religions was a whole lot lower yet. The more power elites have, the less they seem to value other people's lives. History is really quite clear on this.

This is not to say that one should shut up and be grateful for progress – indeed, that is very far from my view.

But there is no reason to believe that the involvement of the masses in politics is the driving force behind racism and sexism or that that these two ills are exclusively perpetrated by the stupid and ignorant (Brexit and Trump voters) against the wishes of a kind and reasoning elite.

Quite the opposite.

If anything, the obvious correlation is that the more people have got involved in politics, the better things have become.

Britain did not decide to colonize India by referendum.

Jeffries, 'Britain's most racist election: the story of Smethwick, 50 years on', *Guardian* (15 October 2014), https://www.theguardian.com/world/2014/oct/15/britains-most-racist-election-smethwick-50-years-on.

* Powell was removed from his post in the aftermath of the speech.

Women were not shoved into the home by referendum.* Mau Mau fighters were not castrated by referendum. The Founding Fathers of the United States were not less racist than Donald Trump, and even Franklin D. Roosevelt ordered Japanese internment during WWII and failed to allow the MS *St. Louis*, carrying 900 European Jewish refugees attempting to escape the Nazis, to dock in America in 1939.[39]

Thus, the equation anti-democrats want to draw –

1 People Disagree With Me
2 That Can Only Be Because They Are Unreasonably Motivated by Racism and Sexism
3 This Is an Emergency
4 Racists and Sexists Have to Be Stopped from Affecting Politics
5 If that Means Curtailing One-Person, One-Vote Democracy, So Be It

– is *not* backed up by the facts. Indeed, British people were arguably a lot more racist and sexist when they agreed via referendum to stay in the EU back in 1975 (some of them having voted for Mr. 'If you want a n***** for a neighbour' just ten years earlier). We can't, in other words, determine a clear link between levels of racism and sexism and support (or lack thereof) for anti-democrats' preferred policies and candidates. There is no reason to believe that people generally reject anti-democratic policies not because they disagree with

---

* Although they were, in some sense, kept there in Switzerland between 1959 and 1971 after a failed referendum to allow them to vote in federal elections – developments are never entirely linear.

those policies on substantive grounds, but from irrational motives of sexism and racism.

And even if that were true, looking back, I think it becomes obvious that the time to throw the idea of majority rule overboard because of fears of racism and sexism is definitely not now. In fact, there was probably never a good time to do so. The popularity of the Ku Klux Klan in the 1920s, back when the group was actively lynching people, was *not* a good reason to get rid of democracy. Quite the opposite. In fact, we know very well what happened in countries that did get rid of democracy at the time.

So panicking about racism and sexism to the point where one feels the need to offload responsibility is a tempting narrative and one designed to play off people's better nature, but ultimately it doesn't hold water, and is really just a vicious attack on political rights under the guise of caring for the vulnerable.

Don't fall for it.

Objection Two: People Are Too Stupid for Democracy

Another favourite anti-democrat talking point is people's ineptitude at answering questions about political trivia. It's a stock trope of hyperventilating newspaper articles and panicking academics, and it always takes the same line, screeching about how many people cannot identify their State senator,[40] don't know who Mikhail Gorbachev is[41] or are unable to name the three branches of government.[42] They may not know what party controls Congress, what the Cold War 'was about' or what the political label 'liberal' means. They may be unaware of how much the federal budget decreased or the proportion of the national budget spent on international aid.[43] As if that weren't bad enough, the masses show a greater ability to recognize the faces of people who are frequently on television rather than those of Supreme Court justices (who work in an atmosphere where cameras are forbidden),[44] and may not even know which party their elected representatives belong to.[45]

Despite their endless repetition, such findings are continuously greeted among anti-democrats with a kind of gleeful shock horror: *Look how dumb everyone is!*

If you can't name your Senator, so this logic goes, how could you *possibly* make a decision on what form the nation's healthcare system should take or whether the government should sign a climate change treaty? Surely, such ignorance is itself a disqualifier, and proves that decisions must be left in the hands of the knowledgeable.

But – as usual – the self-appointed great and good have been far too eager to interpret some superficial stats as rock-solid confirmation of their own worst suspicions.

First, there is the rather obvious question: why *are* these little factoids so important?

Do they serve any purpose, or, indeed *the* purpose of leading to better decision-making?

Does a person's ability to cold recall whether their governor is a Democrat or a Republican or to instantly recognize Baroness Hale, President of the UK's Supreme Court, should they bump into her at the pub, really translate into superior know-how when it comes to deciding what kind of school they want their kids to go to, or somehow add to their views on the pros and cons of financial regulation?

Not really, no.

Complex problem-solving and weighing up different options under a multitude of variables (as is required in political decision-making) does not actually have very much to do with the ability to call to mind some anodyne facts. Indeed, the intense focus on trivia as an acceptable barometer of political capability is a peculiarly anti-democrat phenomenon.

The gap between memorizing a few facts in school and applying that knowledge to solve real-world problems is a well-known one, not least because the real world is rather tricky and thus hard to reduce to disconnected facts.

It's easy to slip up here and even anti-democrats do.

They may, for example, be able to rattle off 'executive, legislative and judicative' as the three branches of government, but they often struggle to apportion precise competencies to each branch.* Gerard Delanty, for example, one of the professors whom I cited earlier as storming against the foolishness of the majority and demanding that their will on Brexit be overturned, lets us know that: 'When direct democracy is used, which is rare, it is overseen by parliament in order to ensure that it does not undermine the fundamental assumptions of democracy and the constitutional rights of individuals.'[46]

That is news indeed, considering that parliaments – the legislative branch of government – are not tasked with ensuring that citizens' rights are not 'undermined'

---

* Bryan Caplan, for example, refers multiple times to Supreme Court justices as 'subordinates' of the President who appoints them (Caplan, *The Myth of the Rational Voter*, note 3, ll. 3231–3239), which is not only to entirely misstate the official textbook relationship between executive and judiciary, but to considerably overstate the *realpolitische* relationship between them as well.

by democracy. After all, practically every law that par-
liamentarians pass infringes on citizens' rights, whether
that be their freedom to drive their cars at 150 miles
an hour down the motorway or to set off fireworks in
their backyards. It is the prerogative of the judiciary (or
'courts' as they are generally known) to determine the
legality of those infringements and ensure that constitutional rights are not completely undermined. That is the
case in *representative* democracy. When direct democracy is used in many countries, the purpose is often to
determine what the constitutional rights of citizens *are*
in the first place. Courts may then proceed to interpret
those rights, and legislators may legislate in accordance
with them, but there is no further appeal from the people's decision on the contents of those rights. Citizens
decide what the law is, and institutions are constrained
by that – not the other way around.

Now, to give him the benefit of the doubt, this was
probably just a muddled statement on Delanty's part,
but it points up a fundamental flaw in anti-democrat
reasoning: just as knowing how a car works in theory
and being able to drive one are two different skill sets,
so it doesn't help anyone to know empty bits of trivia
if they don't *also* know how to use that knowledge in
precise, concrete terms. Thus, even if more people could
rattle off 'legislative, executive and judicative' as the
three branches of government, it wouldn't tell us anything at all about their capabilities in terms of interacting
with those institutions, which is often more complicated,
but also easier to intuit. If one asked an average person
where they should go if their rights were being infringed,
for example, chances are they'd say 'the court', even if
they don't know what the term 'judiciary' means.

This is because we don't *think* in ways that are easily measured by simple fact recalls, but rather in ways that rely far more on prompts, continuous interaction with the environment and accessing information from other people.[47] Humanity, in other words, is basically a hive mind that is constantly in contact with its varied members and the environment.[48] That facilitates dealing with problems without having to completely understand them. Ask someone how to fix a bike in the abstract and they probably won't know what to tell you; put a bike in front of them and chances are they'll manage.[49] That's because we tend to glean information *as needed* from things themselves (e.g., the bike).

We do the same with other people. Sometimes, we even mentally assign a specific person to remember things for us. In one experiment, researchers found that only three months into a steady romantic relationship, each partner was already automatically focusing on topics that he or she had more expertise in (computer software, for example, or financial investments), while the other partner was increasingly tuning out whenever those topics were mentioned in the secure knowledge that that information was now stored in an accessible spot (their partner).[50]

And we don't just rely on our significant other to calculate compound interest or help us find our wallets. We extend this interdependency to the human race in general.

Cognitive scientists Steven Sloman and Philip Fernbach tested this by conducting an experiment that involved showing three mock newspaper clippings to subjects. Each clipping briefly dealt with the discovery of a new kind of rock without giving the reader any real information except the rather unusual characteristic that it glowed. The first clipping claimed that scientists completely understood the new rock; the second clipping claimed that scientists did not understand the new rock; the third claimed that DARPA (an American military research facility) completely understood the new rock, but that they were keeping the information confidential.

The subjects tended to rate their *own* understanding of the mystery rock the highest when shown news clipping one (scientists understood the rock), and lowest when shown news clipping three (DARPA understood it, but wasn't telling anyone what it knew).[51] This indicates that as long as people feel that knowledge exists in a communal pool, and they are confident that they can utilize it at need, then they do, in a sense, know it without the need to immediately personally investigate. After all, they are highly unlikely to be called upon to undertake any task involving a new kind of rock anytime soon.

And while it may all be highly interesting to political scientists, for most people a lot of political trivia fits into this same category. Indeed, the anti-democrats themselves make no case as to why it would be important, or even just useful, for voters to know the names or party affiliation of representatives off the tops of their heads. They merely assume that it is a proxy for political capability. But just as you can count on your significant other to remember your brother-in-law's phone number or the name of that restaurant you both loved, one thing is certain: you can count on politicians to make sure that you know *their* name right when it's most relevant – just before you make the X on a ballot paper. Some people would say it's the *only* thing you can count on them for.

Thus, the need to know, for example, the name of one's State Senator or MP at any given time is hard to see.

Just as, post-graduation, one gradually forgets how to calculate the volume of a cone, so name-and-date trivia tends to shrivel away for lack of actual application. If one needed such information, one could find it; if one were to have a motive for retaining it, one would do so. But generally speaking these circumstances do not obtain.

When they do – in other words, when researchers conduct political surveys under circumstances that incentivize respondents to make an effort and give them the opportunity to access information – accuracy rates improve remarkably. Researchers Arthur Lupia and Markus Prior found that offering people just one dollar for every answer they got right on a survey led to an 11 per cent increase in correct answers, while giving people twenty-four hours to respond increased correct responses by 18 per cent. When respondents were given twenty-four hours to respond *and* one dollar for each correct answer, correct responses increased by 24 per cent.[52] Thus, in situations that more closely approximate real life, we already see people performing better, even on trivia, than anti-democrats would have one believe.

And when experiments more closely mimic real life, people also, it turns out, don't fare too badly on the anti-democrats other main objection – consistency.

In fact, a 1998 study showed that ordinary people rarely committed logical inconsistencies when they were asked to choose between different interlocking national policies that primarily concerned budgeting.[53] In this study, Americans were asked two hundred questions over a forty-five-minute period. Buried in those two hundred questions were twelve 'pairs' that asked respondents for their preferences on lowering/raising taxes; providing social services like Medicaid; paying off the national deficit; and military spending. These pairs of questions were asked in different ways so that it was possible for people to answer them inconsistently. However, not only were Americans overwhelmingly absolutely consistent on what they wanted across all twelve questions (only 12 per cent of respondents made an inconsistent choice even once, despite the fact that the questions were separated by up to twenty minutes of unrelated chatter on different topics), when they were given the chance to review and amend their responses, they often caught their own inconsistencies and corrected them.[54] When it comes to picking policies in scenarios that mimic real life, by asking people to select actual policy choices, even ones set in complex relationships to each other, people demonstrably know what they are doing and are able to functionally use their knowledge.

In recent years this evidence has only been bolstered by the hundreds of successful participatory budgeting exercises – in which voters allocate funding to various projects directly – around the world. These projects (which we will return to briefly in Part III) show extremely high levels of both consistency and practicality in citizen decision-making.

Success, in the real world, is largely determined by our ability to continually assess circumstances around us and keep reacting to them bit by bit to try to stay ahead of the curve. It's a different kind of knack, but one we've definitely got.

Anti-democrats, however, remain hell-bent on testing

people for the wrong skill set – knowing facts that political scientists think are important – and then castigating them for their failure. Achen and Bartels cursorily dismissed the 1998 study cited above on the rather off-base grounds that many people were unaware that Bill Clinton reduced the American federal budget deficit in the 1990s.[55] They ask (rhetorically): 'Could people so blatantly unaware of such a salient and politically consequential fact possibly make budget policy choices with reasonable discernment?',[56] completely failing to recognize the fact that the obvious answer according to the study, and thus according to the observable evidence, is 'yes, they can'.

Anti-democrat findings on people's sketchy trivia skills would only be relevant if they could show that in actual decision-making exercises this affected their ability to make reasonable or consistent decisions.

But this is not the case. There is no more evidence to believe this than there once was to believe that the poor, women and ethnic minorities were too stupid to vote. All the anti-democrats have are shallow tests and a history of interpreting results in the most negative light possible towards the intended victims. Unconvincing.

Objection Three: There's No Point to Democracy Because People Don't Know What Is Good for Them Anyway

So, we've seen that people aren't all that evil, and that there is no reason to believe that they are particularly stupid in any way that substantively impacts on decision-making. This brings us to our third anti-democrat argument: that people simply don't know what is good for them. Indeed, one of the most common threads of the anti-democrat line is that people don't *bother* to learn about politics, because they realize that their vote is but one of meaningless millions and that it is unlikely that their particular vote will decide the fate of an election.[57] Due to this morbid lack of interest, 'the people' acquire an ignorance so profound that they don't even know what is good for them (although anti-democrats of various stripes are always willing to help them out in that regard).

Even at the surface level, it is a rather strange hypothesis (despite running as a staple of academic doctrine under the term 'rational ignorance').

In Douglas Adam's sci-fi classic, *The Hitchhikers' Guide to the Galaxy*, the obsessive inventor Trin Tragula, driven to distraction by his wife's continual pleas to try to 'have some sense of proportion', invents a machine known as the Total Perspective Vortex, which forces people to recognize the universe and their place in it in accurate perspective. When Mrs Tragula is hooked up to the machine, the total perspective she is subjected to annihilates her brain. Every other person who steps into the Vortex and is confronted with their true insignificance suffers a similar fate, and it eventually finds use as an instrument of torture and execution. As Douglas Adams himself put it, 'if life is going to survive in a Universe of this size, then the one thing that it cannot afford to have is a sense of proportion'.[58]

It seems unlikely that people don't bother to learn about political issues because they've spent some time in the Total Perspective Vortex and miraculously not only survived, but are still capable of agonizing over which flavour of Pop Tarts to buy.

Most people, in fact, don't complain about the statistical insignificance of their vote, because they are willing to recognize that everyone gets an equal say, which limits their own personal importance. Instead, they complain about the efficacy of voting in general, because no one is listening to them or any of the other people like them.

Contrary to anti-democrat doctrine (and leaving aside the kind of gerrymandering vote-discounting dark arts that are not very well known and to which anti-democrats are not referring here),[59] every vote *does* influence the outcome of the election, whether it is the first vote to be counted or the last, just as every snowflake on a tree branch contributes to it cracking, not just the last one to land. Only a megalomaniac would believe that it would be necessary for their vote to be a tie-breaker in an election for it to count.

Far from viewing themselves as meaningless drones staring into the grim maw of infinity or insisting that only a tie-breaking vote has any worthwhile impact, I've known people to cast a vote with the explicit purpose of negating the vote of someone they disagree with (often a friend or relative blissfully unaware of the grim vendetta being visited upon them at the ballot box) and professing themselves fully satisfied with that outcome. I've met people who happily cast votes for candidates they think don't have a prayer just to 'support them'. I've also met people who profess no interest in politics, that politicians are all liars, and that nothing will change. But I've yet to meet *one person* who has ever even expressed *any view at all* on the statistical significance or insignificance of their vote. Indeed, as Adams observed, if there is one rational irrationality people seem hardwired to believe in, it is that they personally are important and that unlikely things are, in fact, likely to happen to them. They play the lottery, after all.

However, anti-democrats cling to the narrative of futility-induced ignorance, because it allows them to interpret disagreement between what they want and what people in general want, not as a case of genuine differences of opinion, but as the ignorant herd's inability to know its own best interests. It turns out, this is quite a simple concept. If a person agrees with the anti-democratic author, they know their own best interests. But if they disagree with him, they are wallowing in darkness.

As you might expect, the contortions that anti-democrats go through to 'prove' this are fascinating.

For Bryan Caplan, a libertarian whose cover illustration on *The Myth of the Rational Voter* is a crowd of sheep (just to drive home his point for the illiterate masses one assumes) and who quotes Adam Smith with an intensity normally reserved for the Bible during Sunday-morning evangelism, a failure to accept laissez-faire economics is *ipso facto* proof of not knowing your own best interests and thus of being too stupid for democracy.*

According to Caplan, there can be no clearer proof of the ignorance of 'the people' than the fact that they are prone to what he sees as biases in their views about the economy, biases for the existence of which Caplan claims to offer 'robust empirical evidence'.[60] However, the standard for 'empirical evidence' in Caplan's world falls a little short of what I would personally be willing to describe as 'robust'.

---

* A view shared by Ilya Somin and Jason Brennan.

For example, he claims that 'the people' are unfit for democracy because they focus too much on the profit-making motives of business and 'neglect the discipline imposed by competition',[61] failing to mention numerous cartels, such as the banks that worked together to rig interest rates and foreign exchange markets and were eventually fined billions by the European Union after the free market remarkably failed to 'discipline' them;[62] private waste collectors carving up different territories to avoid competition in Ireland;[63] or grocery stores fixing the price of bread in Canada for over a decade.[64] It's unclear whether Caplan's libertarian beliefs would lead him to the conclusion that if banks did not need licences than the market would function better or similar, because instead of dealing with some of the more obvious objections to his claims, he uses a typical academic strategy: he backs up his claim – which is that people focus too much on the profit-making motives of business and neglect the discipline imposed by competition – with a footnote that leads to a long, impressive-looking list of literature. That's where the reader is meant to stop. If all those books prove Caplan's contention that people are biased against markets and therefore *unable* to make sound policy choices, well what do you know, right?

This is one of the cheap conjuring tricks that anti-democrats frequently use to create their little illusions.

Now, as fate would have it, my parents were heavily into Dr Seuss – or at any rate, bought us all his books. And while, even back then, I dismissed *The Cat in the Hat* as a vulgar commercial venture, I did appreciate the good doctor's more avant-garde work. One of these nursery school classics (*On Beyond Zebra*) had the refrain, 'some people stop at the Z, but not me!' before setting off into imaginary alphabet territory. For some reason, I took to that slogan as heartily as I took to the challenge of eating my bread butter side down. And Caplan's footnote about market bias was intended to be an inquiry-curtailing Z if I ever saw one.

So I skipped over to a library and looked up every book and article in that footnote. Want to know what *wasn't* in those sources? Actual evidence that people are biased against markets. The works cited range from articles coauthored by Caplan himself making the same bald statements he does in his book,[65] to libertarian economists urging each other to throw themselves into politics even if everyone else *does* think they're crazy,[66] to typical railing about lack of innovation in public enterprise,[67] to why we have to accept that it might just not pay off to regulate workplace safety.[68] The most convincing of all the numerous works cited, and it was not terribly convincing, started from the argument that people, having evolved from small tribal bands, could not intuitively understand the vast plane of modern economics.[69] Most of the literature stemmed from before the turn of the millennium, much of it from the 1970s and 1980s – back when neoliberalism was in its infancy and the evidence for the downsides of deregulation hadn't mounted to its current heights.

So, on first appearance, the big, fat footnote made it look like there was a lot of back-up for the claim that people are too focused on the profit-making nature of business to be able to make sound decisions. But chug on past that Z and it's just a collection of general textbooks, libertarian pep talks and outdated articles. One shouldn't complain about people's ignorance, when one is seeking to take advantage of it oneself. But fairness is not something anti-democrats excel at, and it is one of their more common strategies to try to invoke a load of authority to shut people up even if that authority doesn't really have anything to do with their claim.

Some of Caplan's other claims, that people are unreasonably biased to see profits as 'a hand-out' rather than 'a quid pro quo', or that the rich are just providing something people will pay for,[70] don't even have footnotes.

Finally he rounds off on the subject of biases that preclude sound decision-making, and thus the principle of majority rule, by telling us that there is a 'conspiracy theory that is as populous as it is bizarre: capitalists join forces to keep wages at the subsistence level'.[71] According to Caplan, that people would be willing to entertain such thoughts is proof of nothing but 'bias' because 'there are literally millions of employers in the First World ... Just imagining the logistics of such a plot is laughable.'[72]

However, as Caplan is surely aware, employers are organized into numerous umbrella associations, many of which in turn belong to just a handful of major employers' organizations, for example the Confederation of European Business (also known as BusinessEurope) or Keidanren in Japan, as well as being organized into syndicates and private industry groups focused on pushing their prerogatives through government, such as the European Roundtable of Industrialists or the American Legislative Exchange Council. Thanks to these centralized organizations, the logistics of keeping the playing field tilted in their favour (or, as they would put it, 'staying competitive' and encouraging 'labour flexibility'), are actually quite simple and well documented.[73]

The Terrible Truth

It's pretty amazing to think that a book that just made these claims without any back-up was published by Princeton University Press and called the best political book of the year in the *New York Times* (and this is the tip of the iceberg when it comes to Bryan Caplan's insane statements, which include such gems as: 'One gender often knows more about a field than the other. Economics is a field where men happen to have the advantage ... Men also have more political knowledge than women, and think more like toxicologists' (yes, toxicologists. Google it – if you are a woman, that is; if you are a man, you probably already know); and: 'the rich are not trying to advance upper-class interests'; along with Caplan's musings that the nation cannot possibly be overrun with drugs, because, for unfathomable reasons, no one ever offers *him* any).[74]

But this is how things roll in the anti-democrat world. They *don't* check footnotes or greet strange claims with at least a grain of salt, because if they did the whole house of cards would collapse. It only continues via a willing suspension of disbelief.

But that's just the beginning.

It goes on.

Caplan's 'big idea' centres around so-called 'enlightened preferences'.* A voter's enlightened preferences are what that voter would want if only he or she were less ignorant.

So, you might ask, how does one determine the 'enlightened preferences' of the mere mortal? It's simple. You take a sample of regular people and ask them a

---

* An idea that Caplan credits to Scott Althaus, but which he applies specifically to economic policy.

bunch of questions. Then you take a sample of PhD economists and do the same. Then some interesting maths comes in. For example, average people with an average education might yield a 40 per cent approval rating for free trade, but economist PhDs might have a 90 per cent approval rating of free trade. Caplan awards both levels of education with a certain score; for example, the average person's education might be a '4', but a PhD education might be a '6' – the difference obviously being 2. Caplan then multiples 2 by a certain coefficient obtained from the PhDs' 90 per cent approval rating of free trade and adds that in to the average people's approval rating, thus increasing their apparent approval of free trade.[75] This effectively shifts the answers of regular people towards the answers of economists.

Caplan views this as gold-plated proof that economists are not biased, since once the regular people have been suitably 'enlightened', it turns out that their opinions start to converge with those held by economists, even if their gender, social status, etc. remain the same. That can only mean that the economists were right all along. It seems to have escaped Caplan that there is literally no other possible outcome of this experiment, which explicitly amounts to bending the answers of one group to match the answers of the other group. This would happen regardless of the criteria used. If one were to divide the respondents into men and women and then change women's answers to match the answers they would have given 'if they were men', one would also see a convergence after women had been suitably 'masculated'.

The mere fact that people may be influenced by different factors in their views doesn't contribute anything to understanding which of those views are 'right' or 'wrong'. Perhaps people who don't have a PhD in economics just don't understand that, despite 40 years of growing inequality and rampant unpunished corruption in the financial sector, any second now a wonderful era of universal prosperity is about to dawn. Or perhaps many economists are inculcated to follow doctrine in a manner that blinds them to observational data in a self-reinforcing groupthink that has little contact with the outside world. Based on Caplan's experiment, both explanations are possible.

Yet based on his arbitrary determinations of what is right and wrong, Caplan explicitly endorses overruling the majority for its own good.[76]

And concerningly, mainstream elites like Achen and Bartels are only too happy to agree that 'even policies that are unambiguously preferred by a majority of citizens to the status quo may or may not be good policies in the broader sense of comporting with citizens' interests'.[77]

But could Achen and Bartels' views on what majority interests are be different than Caplan's? Could it just be that different people have different views? Are there perhaps equally valid ways of viewing the world that can't be easily reconciled, but that don't necessarily mean that the people holding them are unfit to vote?

Be warned: that is exactly the kind of common-sense thought that outs you for a peasant, unfit for these rarified thought experiments.

In Caplan's world there is one good: the free market. And in the Absolutistan inhabited by Achen and Bartels, that one good is the respectable elite, because: 'Elite culture is usually (though not always) [and they are living proof of this] less susceptible to nutty or dangerous visions.'[78]

While for free market anti-democrats, the indisputable proof of people not knowing what is good for them lies in their unashamed propensity for joining unions, supporting affirmative action, and a crazy suspicion that automation leads to job losses, for liberal anti-democrats, you need only look at the degree to which the peon tries to avoid tax, a characteristic solely attributable to their inability to understand that tax is in their own best interests.

You'll find 'liberal' anti-democrats harping on two particular examples here: property tax referenda in Illinois and Proposition 13 in California.

In Illinois, in some cases, a referendum is required in order to increase property taxes by more than changes in the Consumer Price Index or 5 per cent (whichever is the lesser amount).[79] According to a study on the subject, in districts without such referenda, fire services funding increased by $1.50 per paying unit during the study timeframe, while in districts with referenda, spending still increased, but only by $1.07 – a difference of forty-three cents.[80] The amount of property tax that each household paid for fire services was on average $25.80 annually. Thus, the amount of property tax paid for fire services increased across the board, but in districts with referenda, property taxes paid for fire services increased by a little over 4 per cent, whereas in districts without referenda they increased by just under 6 per cent.[81] This, according to anti-democrats, led to an increase in fire response times, and, since fires are dangerous, by withholding this minuscule amount of money from the tax collector, those Illinoisans who had referenda in their areas were shooting themselves in the foot. People in Illinois may well be capable of tying their own shoes (and then again they may not be, let's not get crazy here), but they *don't know* apparently that their taxes pay for things like fire trucks or understand the connection between an adequate number of fire hydrants and their house burning down, which is why they need experts to make these decisions for them.

As the smoking gun of voter irrationality that the anti-democrats are seeking, it has to be said, this less-than-fifty-cents tax difference lacks a certain something.

And that's before you learn one or two other things.

The first is how high property taxes are in Illinois. My initial reaction on reading this study was that forty-three cents would be a tiny proportion of my own couple of hundred euros property tax bill. But since the USA has a reputation as a low-tax country, I thought I'd better revert to my 'going beyond Z' motto and check it out. Contrary to my expectations, I learned that home-owners in Illinois pay *a lot* more property tax than I do. Indeed, property taxes have been a notorious political football between the state's two major parties for decades, and have come to be used as an inadequate substitute for other forms of tax.[82] That's why property taxes in Illinois are currently the second highest in the USA. The tax bill for an average home can easily come in at around $2,000–$3,000 a year, with rates in some neighbourhoods topping $6,000 a year.[83] That makes it hard to believe that the ignorant mob is making a real stand over 43 cents' worth of fire service.

In addition to that, *before* referenda were instituted, fire response times throughout most of Illinois 'were already three times higher [i.e. longer] than the national standard, when government officials were in charge', so the fact that 'they increased by about 10 per cent after voters gained control over revenue growth'[84] doesn't quite do it as grounds for complete panic. It would seem that government officials were already screwing up just fine on their own and the difference between a fire service that is 300 per cent over the standard response time, as opposed to one that is 330 per cent over the standard response time and costs you forty-three cents less doesn't even seem to fall within the parameters of the perceptible.

All things considered, at the time of the study Illinois simply had substandard fire services. Either these services were underfunded before referenda were instituted and that is the general reason for their untimeliness, or they were run inefficiently and it should have been entirely possible to reform them and get a fire service that actually arrived on time for the same amount of money. There were obviously some deeper structural issues in this sector that the referenda did not affect either way to any appreciable degree.

And little has changed – Illinois and Chicago, its largest city, are bywords for corruption in American politics (Illinois governors have a 50 per cent incarceration rate), and the state imposes a fairly high tax burden on its residents yet seems to perpetually struggle to make ends meet. Today, its referenda on service spending often involve higher stakes – a referendum on a tax increase of $100 for an average household would be typical. Some referenda, which still often pertain to fire services, are accepted, others rejected. However, Illinoisans themselves seem fully aware that the problems go deeper – while most approval and rejection rates of referenda come in at the 50–65 per cent mark, an (advisory) referendum prohibiting businesses with state contracts to engage in campaign funding passed with 95 per cent of votes in favour.[85] Illinois has certainly suffered from poor government, but nothing seems to warrant the belief that this is solely because Illinoisans are incapable of assessing their own best interests and need to be protected by higher authority – quite the opposite.

But that doesn't stop the anti-democrats from putting the same argument on repeat to explain how Californians brought the devastation of the 1991 Oakland fire on themselves.

According to Achen and Bartels, people in the area hit by the Oakland fire (a major wildfire that destroyed three thousand homes and led to twenty-five deaths in a San Francisco suburb in 1991) 'probably' voted in favour of Proposition 13 in 1978. Proposition 13 – a beloved topic among anti-democrats far and wide – limited California's property tax rates to 1 per cent of a home's value, and restricted increases to 2 per cent a year, unless ownership changed. Voters endorsed Proposition 13 back in the time of 8-tracks and bellbottoms primarily due to the fact that inflation and rising property values were making it difficult for retirees to meet their tax bill and thus to remain in their homes.[86] Despite the fact that California was running a budget surplus in the billions,[87] and therefore didn't technically need to collect property taxes at a rate that was running at 52 per cent above the national norm and increasing by as much as 30 per cent a year in some areas, its legislature had repeatedly failed to take action on this point.[88] The situation, at least for some people, was quite dire, and while Prop. 13 may not be a complete solution to housing policy in California (and indeed, was not intended to be), it did achieve its purpose – homeowners, particularly the elderly, were not priced out of their homes. Today, property taxes in California are somewhat under the median American rate, coming in at thirty-four out of fifty states,[89] while state income and sales taxes have been increased to make up the difference.[90] Indeed, via Prop. 30 in 2012, Californians voted to increase tax on incomes over $250k a year, a measure that affects approximately 1.5 per cent of the population and that brings in about $6 billion of revenue annually. One could argue that via Prop. 30, Californians have found a more equitable way of raising revenue than increasing property taxes by an average of nearly $500 on each of the state's thirteen million housing units (the amount that would be necessary to make up $6 billion).

Nonetheless, the anti-democrats insist on seeing Prop. 13 in a purely negative light, and some claim that this foolish law is responsible for the destruction of approximately 3,000 homes in the 1991 Oakland fire, as, in their view, the lack of property tax revenue prevented fire services from being sufficiently prepared.

What they don't mention is that the Oakland fire started in close urban proximity and was fanned by 100km/h winds – that would be winds moving at about the same speed you're going when you're driving down a highway. In neighbouring, more socially minded Canada,[91] a similar fire destroyed 2,400 homes in the Albertan oil town of Fort McMurray in 2016 for the simple reason that it is a lot harder than one might think to stop flames being driving by 100km/h winds. Indeed, some of the major complications of the

Oakland fire, which was generating such heat that it was igniting the tops of telephone poles ahead of the line of fire, included: roofing materials and landscaping used in the area were highly flammable; the fire burned through the power lines that pumped water from reservoirs; and, due to varying fire hydrant connectors, neighbouring forces were delayed in bringing assistance. According to the official report: 'As long as the wind was present, the fire was going to continue to spread, no matter what strategy and tactics were used and no matter how much equipment and how many firefighters were there to try to stop it. The fire was contained only when the wind changed.'[92] That truth is underlined by the fact that the Oakland fire was started by a previous blaze reigniting. That earlier fire had been contained and firefighters were still *on site* when it flared up again.[93] In other words, a firefighting force was, to all intents and purposes, already standing on top of the fire when it reignited and immediately called for back-up, a reaction time far beyond anything taxes could ever buy.

There were, in other words, many factors at play in the Oakland fire that had nothing to do with tax cuts, and it is therefore highly uncertain that any realistic spending increase could have significantly mitigated the damage.

But even if one *were* to accept that Proposition 13 (and Proposition 13 alone) prevented proper fire preparedness, one has to ask: how *would* it have helped retired California homeowners who were in danger of losing their homes *in 1978* to have to pay higher taxes and thus perhaps lose their homes, to know that an infinitesimally small fraction of those homes (three thousand out of a total eleven million households in California)[94] *might* not burn in 1991 if only they would agree to part with an unaffordable sum of money right then? Some of those individuals were likely *dead* by the time Doc Martens, Nirvana and the Oakland fire rolled around. And while you can't get much in the way of insurance should you be unable to meet your tax obligations (especially once you retire), it's pretty standard (and thus affordable) to insure your home against fire, a hazard that exists quite apart from firestorms.

So even if voters were made to believe that there would be about a one in five thousand chance of their house burning down in a firestorm thirteen years in the future,* they might well think, 'That's lovely, but there is a much higher chance of me losing my home if my property tax keeps going up, not to mention a certain chance that I may be dead by 1991, and also: I'm already insured!'

Thus, neither on the facts nor on the theory does Proposition 13 stack up as evidence that voters don't know what is good for them.

Yet anti-democrats often refer to it as the ultimate proof of just that,[95] claiming, for example: 'Direct democracy had overruled the judgement of fire professionals with horrific results',[96] despite the fact that no one 'overruled' the judgement of fire professionals (Prop. 13 wasn't about fire safety); there was probably little that an increased tax could have done to make a major impact on controlling the fire (even supposing it

---

* The chance of a California resident's home being burned down in the Oakland fire was *ca.* 0.027 per cent – by comparison there's a 25 per cent that you'll manage to start at least one fire in your home that warrants calling the fire department.

had been used for those purposes); and it is not terribly likely that even had Californian voters been able to see into the future and find out all about the Oakland fire down to the last detail that very many of them would have changed their votes.

It is far easier to draw a connection between elite action (or lack thereof) on wars, gun violence, prison policy, mental health provision and the negative consequences that derive from all of the above than it is to draw one between the popular vote for Proposition 13 and the Oakland fire.

The evidence for the fact that the people themselves are not acting in their own best interests can only be sustained by ignoring what prima facie very much appears to be in their interests (things like having a home, for example, or getting weekends off work) and replacing it with the anti-democrats' harsh prescription of what is 'really' good for them (apparently having to move in with their children for the greater good of the state budget surplus). The chief fault of the people, it would appear, lies only in a certain lack of love for pointless masochism.

I rest my case.

On to the next thing, because with anti-democrats there is always a next thing.

Objection Four: People Are Just Too Crazy for Democracy to Work

The anti-democrats' final go-to strategy for delegitimizing majority rule is to convince the world that democracy can only work in a society of rational beings (Vulcans,

53

according to some),* and since this description does not apply to the vast majority of humans, their political participation must, somehow, be contained.

One of the major arms of this argument is that people allegedly vote retrospectively; that is, they mentally 'grade' politicians at the end of their term in office and if they think they have done well they vote for them again, but if they think they have done poorly, they vote for someone else.

Under normal circumstances, this mainstay political science doctrine is not all that problematic. It more or less stands to reason that if a voter votes for an incumbent politician then that voter is somewhere between fully and barely confident in that politician's abilities, or, failing that, not particularly tempted by their rivals. It's a low bar and the calculation underlying this decision could have hundreds of variables – it is, after all, largely subjective and dependent on the value that each voter places on specific policies or outcomes, what they believe the duties of a politician are or should be, the level of integrity they feel the politician has shown during their term, and who the competition is. Any vote could express a thousand different shades of approval or disapproval on any given point. Whatever the ultimate cause, however, voters make their choice on what the most sensible option is for them personally based on what they regard as the pros and cons of each option, taking past performance into consideration to some degree, depending on its importance to them.

So far, so normal.

---

* Jason Brennan uses the term Vulcan to describe the fully rational, while all others are either 'hobbits', or 'hooligans'.

However, some political scientists flip this around and attribute to themselves the one true knowledge of each politician's successes and failures; what they are responsible for and what they are not responsible for. Based on this, they issue a kind of mental 'report card' on each politician, which they consider to be an impartial assessment of that individual's performance and thus an objective indicator of whether said politician should be re-elected. If for any reason their report card and 'the people's' report card on any given politician don't match up, then that can only be because people are making not *subjectively different*, but actually irrational choices based on wildly incorrect, thoroughly unreasonable and utterly unfair assessments of the politician's performance.

The book *Democracy for Realists*, written by Professors Christopher Achens and Larry Bartels, recently explored this concept in great detail.

The most famous, lauded, praised and quoted example of voter irrationality in their book is the claim that voters change their votes based on arbitrary, uncontrollable events like shark attacks, because on some level they *literally* blame incumbent politicians for the uncontrollable event having occurred – much, according to Achen and Bartels, like ancient Egyptians once blamed the Pharaoh when the Nile failed to flood.[97]

When other academics and pundits heard this claim, they, by and large, did not scratch their heads and ask: 'are you really sure about that?'

Instead, they lost their minds like a 16-year-old at a Beatles concert.

The finding that people are so hopelessly irrational that they refuse to vote for politicians because they blame them for events like shark attacks has been cited in more than 400 academic papers[98] and uncritically repeated as proof of humanity's unfitness to execute the political participation expected of them at the ballot box everywhere and anywhere from the Brookings Institute,[99] to the Princeton University website,[100] to academic reviews,[101] to a Reuters article musing that 'Obama can take heart that Florida beachgoers haven't suffered from a spate of shark attacks this year'.[102]

The stream of praise that followed the release of *Democracy for Realists* seemed inexhaustible.

One day, it even reached my little ears.

And, I have to say, the whole theory sounded a bit odd to me, because, while I've met some strange people in my life, none of them seemed irrational to the point where they were likely to blame a politician for a shark attack.

So I investigated.

First, the facts of what I shall henceforth term 'Sharknado' in honour of the B-movie series of the same name. Achen and Bartels base their contention that shark attacks affect voting behaviour on a particular historical incident – a freak string of shark attacks that occurred around New Jersey four months before the 1916 American presidential election. This event was major news at the time; the shark, apparently not content with coastal depredations, even swam up a creek 16 miles inland and killed two people there.[103] Unsurprisingly, the prospect of being eaten alive had a sudden and negative impact on beach-based tourism in New Jersey, with a quarter of a million dollars' worth of hotel reservations cancelled in just one week.[104] Confronted with this dilemma, local people took to their boats to hunt the shark,[105] which is thought to have been killed by a fisherman two days after the last attack.[106]

Although the attacks lasted for only two weeks and ceased at a time still four months ahead of the election, Achen and Bartels claim to have discovered that in the townships where the attacks occurred, support for Woodrow Wilson, then running as the incumbent candidate, dropped by 9–11 points compared to where it 'should have been' based on what the 1912 figures were, when Wilson was running for his first term.[107] According to the authors, although a government today might deal with such a situation via unemployment compensation or similar programmes, because these were not regular policy features at the time, voters would not have expected such relief. Thus, the dip in support for Wilson that they identified in New Jersey cannot be explained by voter dissatisfaction with the government's handling of the crisis; it can only be explained by people irrationally punishing Wilson for the shark attacks, something he did not cause and therefore could not have been expected to rectify.[108]

Now – at first glance that sounds insane, but it did possess the dubious merit of saying something anti-democrats love to hear: people are crazy. And that is likely why they chose to blindly repeat and even exaggerate these findings from New Jersey to Timbuktu.

In reality, however, the 'Sharknado' narrative has the structural integrity of a Jenga tower half an hour into the game.

Not only does the underlying data not support it, it intentionally or negligently fails to take into consideration many important political factors in the American electoral system.

For starters, the total number of votes cast in shark-traumatized New Jersey was small[109] and the population was growing rapidly, making comparisons between election years difficult;[110] furthermore, Achen and Bartels made multiple value judgements and far-from-watertight assumptions when deciding how to process their data.[111]

For example, they interpreted the fact that third-party candidate and former Republican President Theodore Roosevelt polled better in the shark-afflicted beach counties than in other parts of the state in 1912 to mean that Wilson should have had more voters to pick up there than in other parts of New Jersey in 1916, rather than assuming that such voters would likely revert to voting Republican in the two-party race of 1916[112] (indeed, New Jersey in general voted Republican for forty straight years with the sole exception of 1912, a year that saw both the first-time candidacy of Woodrow Wilson, then Governor of New Jersey, and a simultaneous exceptionally strong third-party candidacy from Roosevelt).

These kind of value judgements in processing the data showed up later on: when the numbers were examined by two other political scientists, who studied 'every fatal shark attack in US history'[113] 'and county level returns from every presidential election between 1872 and 2012',[114] they found 'no systematic evidence that shark attacks affect elections',[115] regardless of how they ran the data and which variables they used.[116]

In addition to these factors, it is certainly a fly in the ointment of Achen and Bartels's theory that Wilson's vote share dropped by *even greater* percentages in other parts of New Jersey that were not affected by the shark attacks,[117] as well as in other states, culminating in the loss of every state (not just New Jersey) in the northeastern and Great Lakes regions.[118] At the same time, Wilson gained votes in Matawan Borough and Matawan Township, the location of the shark's amazing swim-up-a-creek trick that killed two people – half of all the fatalities and two-fifths of the shark's total victims.[119]

Achen and Bartels attempt to justify the different voting patterns in Matawan Borough and Township on the basis that 'because these two townships were not beach communities, the attacks should not have affected them'.[120] However, this only highlights their strange logic: if only places affected by a drop in tourism are subject to vote alterations, then surely a vote change, even one explicable by shark attack, would mean that voters are not blaming politicians for the attack per se – the irrational behaviour the authors' claim they are exhibiting – but rather for their lost income. Unlike the actual shark attack, lost income was something the government *could* have chosen to deal with, either by attempting to prevent further loss by undertaking measures to kill the shark, or by offering compensation for incurred loss. The demand for government aid may be selfish (and then again it may not be if you are about to go bankrupt), but it is certainly rational.

And that New Jerseyites' main concern lay with government inaction seems fairly certain, since, according to an academic article Achen and Bartels penned on this theme in 2002, during the shark attacks: 'Letters poured into Congressional offices from the affected counties *demanding federal action.*'[121] This would suggest that the people of New Jersey did, rightly or wrongly, expect some sort of help from government on this point, and that they were dissatisfied at the handling of the situation, rather than blaming the shark attack *itself* on Wilson while entertaining no expectations of government aid, as Achen and Bartels suggest.[122] This is all the more so as disaster relief was *not* an unknown concept in the United States at the time of the attacks[123] and locals were, in fact, able to hunt down the shark – a task they may have appreciated government assistance with.

However, Achen and Bartels vacillate between suggesting that New Jerseyites blamed Wilson for the attack itself, and claiming that it was unreasonable and therefore completely irrational for them to expect compensation for their lost income (a value judgement that New Jerseyites seem to have disagreed with).

The more one reads of *Democracy for Realists* and its attendant praise, the clearer it becomes that the real disagreement is over what expectations voters are *allowed to have* of politicians; in other words, which expectations are legitimate (and thus rational) and which are illegitimate (and thus irrational) as determined by the relevant author.

For example, in Achen and Bartels's view, if a politician is not responsible for an event, in the sense of having caused it, and they personally do not believe the politician should have improved the matter, then it is irrational for people to expect the politician to do something about that problem even – and this is crucial – if the politician could do so.

For example, Woodrow Wilson apparently was responsible for failing to successfully mitigate the 1918 flu epidemic, but definitely not for damage incurred by the shark, because it is Achen and Bartels's personal opinion that Wilson's flu performance was lacking, but that his inaction on the shark losses was the correct choice as these were not his responsibility.

Rather than reflecting on the fact that they might also be subjective in their assessments, Achen and Bartels string this out into a theory that elections are negatively affected by all kinds of irrational voter judgements. For example, they claim that incumbent politicians on average suffer a 0.7 per cent drop at the polls during unusually wet or dry weather, while extreme drought or wet spells bring incumbents about a 1.5 per cent drop compared to where they would otherwise have been.[124] In their view, this explains the 2000 presidential election, which took place following unusually dry and wet weather in various parts of the United States. The authors speculate that, based on their hypothesis – that people irrationally expect politicians to take responsibility for the weather itself – adverse meteorology may have cost Democrat candidate Al Gore millions of votes,[125] resulting in his defeat to Republican candidate George W. Bush.

And this is where things get really interesting, because what Achen and Bartels glaringly *fail* to mention – *although they surely know it* – is that Al Gore won the most votes in the 2000 presidential election.

That's right: despite campaigning on the back of a much more charismatic two-term Democratic president (Bill Clinton), and despite Green candidate Ralph Nader taking 2.9 million votes to the left, Gore still won, not one hundred, not one thousand, but *half a million* more votes than his Republican opponent George W. Bush. That means that, despite dry spells, bad hair days, running out of coffee and whatever else could possibly cause one to cast one's vote in an arbitrarily malcontent manner, nearly 3.5 million *more* people voted for candidates to the left of George W. Bush than for him, and that Al Gore – the man campaigning on the incumbent ticket – point blank won more votes than anyone else. Thus, to speculate that Al Gore lost the election because the crazed mob, having mistaken him for some kind of rain god, and holding him personally culpable for the weather, withheld their votes, and that this should cause us to question whether people are *capable* of exercising their democratic functions, is as devoid of practical significance as the idea that rogue New Jerseyites took down Woodrow Wilson over some shark attacks four months before the 1916 election.

And this leads us to the heart of the matter:

If Al Gore did not lose the election because of bad weather, why did he lose it?

The answer is simple: despite winning the most *actual* votes by a significant margin, Gore lost the vote of the electoral college, the institution that was invented to protect American government against the deranged masses by skewing election outcomes via the insertion of an additional, completely unnecessary filter between the people and the outcome.

Oh, the irony.

Rather than even consider this indisputable, easily fact-checkable reason for why both Al Gore and Hillary Clinton lost their presidential campaigns although they both won the *actual* vote, Achen and Bartels *know* that voters are the problem, even though those would be *the very people* who voted in their majority for Al Gore and Hillary Clinton – and for Woodrow Wilson, for that matter, because contrary to the vague impression that Achen and Bartels create, Woodrow Wilson was

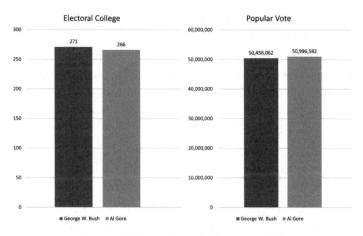

Fig. 1 US Presidential Election 2000

re-elected in 1916 *with a greater percentage of the vote* than he had received in 1912.

That means that the plurality of Americans voted for Achen and Bartels's preferred candidates in 1916, 2000 and 2016. It wasn't them but the electoral system that

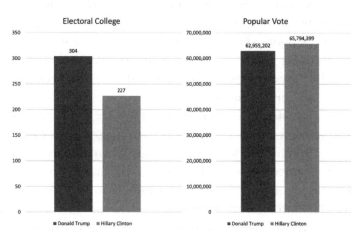

Fig. 2 US Presidential Election 2016

the Founding Fathers designed to prevent populism that prevented the election of Gore and Clinton, and that dramatically reduced Wilson's share of the electoral college vote between his 1912 and 1916 candidacies, despite his increase in vote share.

It also means that even if everything Achen and Bartels said about shark attacks (and everything else) were true (and it isn't), the amount of world history affected would still be zero. In a parallel universe where the 1916 shark attacks hadn't existed, everything would be … exactly the same. That means Sharknado (and its like) aren't just insignificant, they are literally devoid of *any* significance and therefore really lack something as a foundation upon which to build an argument that democracy is not working because people are too irrational.

Instead of acknowledging this basic fact, Achen and Bartels conclude by letting us know that voters get 'misguided tax policies and disastrous foreign wars' because they 'can't distinguish the effects of shark attacks and droughts from the effects of tax policies and foreign wars'.[126]

But that's not true.

Americans ended up with 'misguided tax policies and disastrous foreign wars' because of the electoral college.

Achen and Bartels ignore this because they are obsessed with their own particularly rigid view of retrospective voting, which seems to *obligate* voters to see certain politicians elected based on Achen and Bartels's assessment of their past performance. If voters fail to meet this obligation, it can only be because voters exercise 'myopic judgement' and tend to unfairly blame politicians for events beyond their control.

Only such an explanation, after all, can 'make sense

of such otherwise perplexing outcomes as Winston Churchill's loss of the British prime minister's office in 1945. He may well have asked, "What? Saving you from death in the concentration camps wasn't enough?" But once victory in Europe was achieved, the voters lost interest in that topic. What was on their minds at election time seems to have been the housing shortage ... to which no competent government would have directed money during the war. The voters didn't care. They voted for change.'[127]

But representative democracy does *not* contain any mechanism that would entitle any politician to continue to rule based on past performance no matter how great a job they may have done.

Politics in our society is a contract job that one tenders for ahead of time (like any other contract).

Thus, a failure to vote for Winston Churchill in 1945 does not necessarily imply that any voter (much less all of them) believed that Churchill should have diverted money from the war effort to the housing crisis. It merely expresses that at the time of the election many people believed that another candidate was better positioned to deal with their current priorities. Indeed, public opinion in Britain – which, by the way, had not seen a general election for ten years – was certainly leaning more liberal than, e.g., Winston Churchill, a Conservative politician who could only become prime minister if the Conservative Party in general was victorious. Indeed, many policies that were implemented in Britain following WWII, such as the expansion of a welfare state, were not particularly favoured by the Conservative Party.

Why British voters would 'owe' Winston Churchill the warped tribute of continuing to live in need of housing and social services while exercising imperialist policies many of them did not fully back is hard to see.

This is all the more so as Churchill, inspirational as he was, certainly did not single-handedly save anyone from a concentration camp. A lot of that 'work' was carried out on the ground by the average person in the British armed forces, many of whom paid for it, not in lost elections, but with their lives. So just why people who may have lost relatives defending the nation from invasion owed a particular politician a vote for 'saving them' is hard to see. If anything, such a mind-set reveals a truly vicious determination to ignore the sacrifices and contributions of average citizens and create a fictitiously overblown dependency relationship between them and leading politicians.

Achen and Bartels seem to think elections *should be* about rewarding politicians for past service, and that voters' failure to do so properly is a result of their inferiority and 'myopic' thinking. But when it comes to politics, the reward was already had in getting to run the country.

All in all, Achen and Bartels have a very strange view of elections, and it causes them to come to many strange conclusions about the alleged 'irrationality' of voters, who, far from being crazy, simply have different motivations and opinions than the authors believe they should.

However, obvious as this is, it did not stop the 'respectable elite' from repeating and exaggerating Achen and Bartels's findings, in particular the crowd-favourite Sharknado. One review managed to further inflate their findings to: 'a spate of fatal great white shark attacks around the beaches of New Jersey in the summer of 1916 led to a 10 per cent swing against

Woodrow Wilson in the presidential election later that year',[128] and so much was the story music to academics' ears that when six of them reviewed the book in a prestigious journal,[129] no one questioned the basic account. Instead, several people admired the authors precisely for being able to connect an event as farfetched and preposterous-sounding as shark attacks to electoral outcomes, apparently viewing this as something of an art form.[130]

Achen and Bartels themselves doubled down on their position in a later article clarifying: 'We think of democracy as government *of* the people and *for* the people, but not directly *by* the people. We want democratic leaders to lead. Of course, crackpot dictators and Communist party bosses often justify their rule on the grounds that is it good for the people. This is not what we mean.'[131]

Now, in my humble opinion, when you hear yourself saying something like this: it's time for some self-reflection.

Anti-democrats like to talk a lot about checks and balances when it comes to the will of the people. Just remember what kind of 'checks and balances' they use when the shoe is on the other foot. They take things and run with it just because they like how it sounds and they never worry about how much damage they are doing to other people.

When you hear that your neighbours are too irrational to make decisions or that you should make over your democratic rights to the respectable elite to shelter you from the world, this is the kind of thing it is based on – a pat little story that flies apart in shreds the moment anyone takes a closer look.

And that's that.

To Conclude

What the anti-democrats have managed to put together in the way of proving your, my, and everyone else's ineptitude is basically a big fat zero. The thorough investigation in which every rock has been overturned and every straw, no matter how flimsy, has been grasped has come up empty. I'm sure they'll always find one more little thing and they'll scream and shout that *this one* is finally the *one true proof* for why political equality is a bad idea, but that's their little obsession. It's time we acknowledge the obvious: there's nothing to these claims. Really. Truly. Nothing.

There is no reason to believe that we are currently delving humanity's most rock-bottom levels of racism or sexism or that people are too stupid to vote. Nothing out there particularly demonstrates that people are so irrational as to be unable to differentiate between shark attacks and wars and there's zero evidence that we just can't tell what is in our own best interests. It simply does not stack up.

Anti-democrats' disparaging assessment about the incorrigible romanticism of people who haven't given up on the human race and kowtowed to their natural masters (oddly, other humans) has, as we have seen, less to do with what is true, and much more to do with what anti-democrats *want* to be true. They don't *want* people to be capable of participating, because they don't *want* them to participate.

According to Achen and Bartels, 'Without shirking more immediate and more important obligations, people cannot engage much in well-informed, thoughtful, political deliberation, *nor should they*.'[132] Two of their more influential admirers, Jonathan Rauch and Benjamin Wittes similarly state that 'no one should expect, *or even want*, voters to possess'[133] enough knowledge and sophistication to make reasonable decisions. On the right, Ilya Somin argues that it is better for people to be ignorant about trade, because then government could engage in free trade for their own good,[134] while Brennan argues that, '[i]deally, politics would occupy only a small portion of the average person's attention ... most people would fill their days with ... football, NASCAR, tractor pulls, celebrity gossip and Applebees'.[135]

Take it from the horse's mouth: anti-democrats are not, when it comes down to it, pining for a better, more enlightened humanity; they *want* people to be racist, sexist, ignorant and everything else, because it is the only way to continue to justify their own privileged position into the new interconnected age.

Anti-democrats feel justified in this way of thinking, because, as we have seen, in their view, there is only ever one right way to do things (their own particular preferred way).

This is particularly the case when it comes to the election of Trump and the Brexit vote. In Western countries, as pretty much everyone freely admits, material inequality is increasing dramatically and many people will be worse off than their parents for reasons that are purely political. Unsurprisingly, *most people* would thus like at least some changes to the status quo, and we do live in a society whose official system is government nominally by majority. Rather than acknowledge that many people are seeking alternatives (Trump, Brexit) for an actual reason, or that whenever anyone asks, people keep saying they want change, anti-democrats continue to claim that we live in the best possible reality (indeed, this insistence that the status quo was terrific, despite all evidence to the contrary, was exactly what had such devastating effects for both the British Remain and Hillary Clinton's presidential campaign).

That leaves only two possible explanations: either people in general must be stupid and evil to react so ungratefully to such a terrific reality, or reality is in fact pretty bad, and someone is lying to us. And that would make *them* pretty stupid and evil.

There is no explanation for this fundamental disagreement where no one is stupid and evil. It must be one side or the other. Thus, what is at stake here are entire versions of reality. That is why this argument is so intense.

I'll make things short: as we've seen above, it's not you, it's them.

It's not 'the people', but the anti-democrats who are in the habit of making up cobweb-thin arguments for disenfranchising others and then trying to bully everyone into accepting them as gospel truth.

The onslaught on 'people' is intended to achieve nothing less than to shake one's faith and open up minds to new anti-democratic possibilities. After all, when one sees claims like the fact that people base who they vote for on shark attacks, or the vicious excoriations of not knowing who your backbench MP is, or the continual slandering of anyone who disagrees with one as automatically being a racist, a sexist or an idiot, and one sees this repeatedly proclaimed as the one truth with no further analysis at all, it is bound, sooner or later to have an impact.

But anti-democrats can only achieve this by some measure of duplicity, and not just in relation to bending the 'facts' of their claims.

At this stage of the argument ('people are terrible and stupid') anti-democrats tend to avoid clarity when it comes to the bottom line.

And that bottom line is, if not democracy, then what?

Anti-democrats often try to keep things vague here, arguing, for example, that democracy should not be measured by whether 'policy outcomes track public preferences' but by 'something – as it might seem, almost anything – else'.[136]

This is great for anti-democrats, because in their view government is not about tracking public preferences but about instituting *correct policies*.

It is a common trait to all anti-democrats that they rule out the possibility of legitimate disagreement – that people might value different things, or have different interests. There is one correct way of ordering society – be that libertarian free market capitalism, corporate neoliberalism or anything else – and a political system is simply a procedure to produce that outcome. If that involves restricting equal democratic rights, so be it.

However, as rationality researcher Keith Stanovich put it: 'It is itself a form of irrationality to think that one can discern that one's own worldview is inherently superior to others.'[137] Indeed, study after study has shown that academics (the very people who are supposed to be objective experts) tend to suppress findings they disagree with and to find spurious fault with them,[138] and there is every reason to believe that the smartest and most sophisticated are often also the most biased and resilient to changing their opinions in light of new evidence.[139]

The reason we use majority rule *isn't* to ensure that everyone follows the 'one right way' to live. We use it because in Western democracies we came to the conclusion that there *wasn't* one right way of life for everyone. That's why conflict is embedded in our political system, and having that conflict is what 'politics' is all about. And in the absence of a 'true path' that is *above* politics, we can only choose between majority rule, i.e., what the majority think is right and/or in their interests, and minority rule.

The entire aim of anti-democrats is to build the case for minority rule, although they tend to do this almost exclusively by arguing against majority rule and then leaving the obvious implication hanging in the wind.

For example, one of the key arguments against accepting the Brexit referendum has been that it is 'hard to imagine' a country making such important decisions as Brexit 'by a mere 50 per cent majority'[140] and that '[t]he idea that somehow any decision reached anytime by majority rule is necessarily "democratic" is a perversion of the term'.[141]

But if it is hard to imagine nations making important decisions by a mere 50 per cent plus one majority, surely it is even harder to imagine them making them by a 49 per cent minority, which is literally the only possible alternative.*

Rather than face this fact, anti-democrats generally try to muddy the waters even further by dragging in the presumed 'correct' policy choices.

---

* A decision not to act or to maintain the status quo is, after all, still a decision. For this reason, super-majorities do not give power to a 'supermajority' – they give it to a minority that becomes capable of veto-ing decisions.

The Terrible Truth

A much-loved argument is that 'illiberal' decisions should not be taken by majority, but rather be prevented by some mysterious force (other apparently than the judicial system which, for the most part, is still functioning perfectly fine for this very purpose).

This serves to confuse the entire debate even further. What, after all, do 'liberal' and 'illiberal' even mean? And how can liberal and illiberal values be definitively tied to assessing whether a state is democratic?

Up until only a few decades ago, most Western states had laws that prevented married women from engaging in a variety of activities, such as sitting on juries, holding well-paid jobs or opening bank accounts without their husband's consent. I think that that is illiberal. Does that mean that countries like Canada, Ireland and the Netherlands that had these laws on their books were undemocratic until well into the 1970s?

Many European countries tend to determine citizenship via *ius sanguinis* – that is by right of blood – in ways that can be rather regressive. Are countries like Austria and Switzerland democracies or not?

Some liberal things that are not allowed in the UK include euthanasia, polygamy/polyandry, and most recreational drugs. If the United Kingdom were to hold a referendum on euthanasia, would it need to be 'carefully regulated' so that it does not produce an illiberal result like, e.g., for euthanasia to continue to be illegal?

How would one achieve this regulation to ensure that people vote the way the author would like them to? What kind of regulation is going to turn people liberal and how liberal is liberal enough?

In article after article, anti-democrats fail to complete this thought process, because most people would not accept the logical conclusions of their arguments, namely that a preferred kind of outcome can only be guaranteed via authoritarian rule or, at best, enlightened despotism. Instead, they seek to overwhelm people with a slew of spurious arguments into accepting that they need outside help, help that only the anti-democrats can give, while at the same time muddying the waters with terms like 'liberal' that sound good, but over which there is little consensus as to content, its bearing on democracy, or how such a value system could be imposed under any type of egalitarian government.

I hope that the first part of this book has gone some way to showing this and has given you some reasons as to why you don't need to give up on humanity or democracy just yet in exchange for a slippery promise of ill-defined righteousness.

But anti-democrats don't just talk, they are also already busy working like a tag team to alleviate us from the burdens of self-government, to rescue us, as it were from ourselves. And that bears some thinking about.

Part II

Fixing Politics the Anti-Democrat Way

Notwithstanding their failure to come up with actual evidence of the horrors of one-person, one-vote popular governance, anti-democrats strongly advocate an array of 'solutions' for it. Presumably, once people are convinced of the need to run amok in sheer panic of each other, anti-democrats want to be there with a plan.

Some of these 'solutions' to the alleged downsides of government by the people may seem more palatable than others, but their basic aim is always the same: to ensure an end to political equality and put decisions in the hands of the 'right' people. I'm going to go through these solutions, from the least palatable to the most palatable, so that you can see the similarities build.

Section 1: Assorted Libertarian, Authoritarian and Explicitly Elitist Solutions

Rule by the 'knowledgeable' (Jason Brennan)
There are two things you need to know about Jason Brennan. The first is that he is super-cool. Indeed, as

he lets readers of his book *Against Democracy* know time and again, he drives a sports car, listens to metal bands, flies around the world, and seems to believe that the average 15-year-old should really look up to him. His entire argument is based on the idea that it is deeply unfair for what he views as 'incompetent democracy' to rule his life, as he is an individual and, for some unexplained reason, only individual actions and benefits count. 'Who made *those people* my *boss?*'[1] he asks (referring to democracy), much like teenagers tend to do.

The second thing is that Brennan's single shining contribution to this debate is that, in addition to all of his other suggestions (e.g., more votes for the educated, veto power on laws for the informed), he goes one step farther than everyone else, takes everything to its logical conclusion and argues that ideally no one should have an inherent right to vote. Rather, people should have to *earn* their right to vote, 'if they are deemed ... competent and/or sufficiently well-informed',[2] or as he mentions in a side sentence, if they can pay $2,000 to purchase that right.

This theory is based entirely on one of the premises that we explored in Part I: that people don't bother to learn about politics due to rational ignorance and that they are consequently too stupid and uninformed to vote. Hence, they need to be ruled by the knowledgeable, in order for things to be 'better' and 'more just' – terms Brennan does not find space to explicitly define in more than two hundred pages of writing.

However, one can always read between the lines, and as strange as all these arguments sounded in Part I, it is really here, when one starts to examine their proffered 'solutions', that the biases of anti-democratic thought really start to come into their own, and it becomes apparent that the kind of knowledge *they view* as relevant doesn't necessarily enjoy universal support. High-information voters in Brennan's world, for example, support free trade and increased immigration. They know that Adam Smith (author of the 1776 *Wealth of Nations*) was right about economics all along – indeed, since Brennan's 5-year-old son knows nothing about economics, he is superior to the American public, which is *mistaken* about Smith's economic theories.[3] The knowledgeable are also against price controls, which are 'imprudent, wasteful … immoral and violate citizens' rights'.[4] The knowledgeable also tend to be rich, white middle-aged men, a demographic that is 2.5 times more likely to pass a knowledge test than young, poor black women,[5] because political knowledge is negatively correlated with being black and strongly negatively correlated with being female. However, this demographic schism, which Brennan believes will in fact manifest itself between those with the right to vote and those who will be excluded, is nothing to worry about, because Brennan does 'not want to exclude people or reduce their power, in order to express wrongful contempt or disrespect for any individuals, groups or races'. He only wants to 'produce better, more substantively just policy outcomes'.[6] Therefore, this is merely 'rational statistical discrimination'.[7] One could after all, 'imagine an epistocratic society in which everyone regards one another as having equal status' despite not having equal voting rights.[8]

However, I have to admit – I *can't* quite imagine such a society. Indeed, I don't know of any historical precedent of such a civilization. I only know of societies where, when people don't have an equal say with others, the work and all the other disadvantages tend to get shifted onto them. The society may be more humane, it may be less humane, but that underlying tendency is always there, and I guarantee that if you tried to sell a script to Hollywood about a civilization where many people are excluded from voting on the grounds that they are 'incompetent, ignorant, irrational and morally unreasonable'[9] and thus society must be protected from the 'pollution' of their votes,[10] as Brennan does, but where everyone is still equal, they'd tell you that you are being unrealistic and to come back with something more manageable – like people effortlessly jumping from skyscraper to skyscraper. When I try to imagine a script for this fictitious civilization, this is the best I can come up with:

Paul: 'Hi Rick.'

Rick: 'Hi Paul.'

Paul: 'Where are you off to, Rick?'

Rick: 'I'll be voting, since I passed the test. You, Paul?'

Paul: 'No, Rick. I'm afraid I took a trip to Canada a few months ago, and came back less-than-convinced that price controls are imprudent, wasteful and morally wrong. I've been having some weird thoughts about tax-payer-funded healthcare and education too. I've been thinking so much about this that I forgot to look up the name of my Congressperson, last quarter's GDP and the opening chapter of *Wealth of Nations*.'

Rick: 'Well, Paul, I suppose you're just an incompetent, ignorant, irrational and morally unreasonable person and we'll have to save society from the pollution of

your vote. But I just want you to know – you're still
my equal.'

Paul: 'Thanks, Rick. Hey, do you think you could vote
for someone who is in favour of regulating self-driving
cars. You know, I'm a driving instructor and all ...'

Rick: 'Sorry Paul. That's not my problem. You'll have
to find a way to vote for that yourself. But you are my
equal.'

Perhaps it would all go off more smoothly on Vulcan.
But here on Earth, I feel that previous generations
already lived through eras dominated by white, rich,
middle-aged men, and we know how that turns out.

Voting is not merely a technocratic exercise, nor is
anyone completely 'unbiased' and therefore in a position to decide what is 'best' for other people. We do not
vote to determine the one right way for everyone to live
their lives – there is no such thing. Indeed, it may well be
rational for rich, white middle-aged men to want lower
taxes at the expense of social programmes, for example, but not for young, poor, black women. That does
not make them more knowledgeable. It simply serves
their interests better. But Brennan is perhaps the most
extreme of all anti-democrats in failing to perceive that
his ideas of 'better', 'just' and 'moral' are not universally
shared – and not just because people haven't heard the
wonders of Adam Smith, but rather because they have
different interests.

Even if Brennan were to be correct (and he isn't) that
most voters are 'ignorant, irrational and misinformed
but nice',[11] I'd take that over 'sophisticated, rational and
informed, but evil' any day of the week. Fortunately, we
are spared that choice by the knowledge that voters
actually aren't all that ignorant – they just don't prize

the same information or problem-solve the same way as anti-democrats think they should.

So – give up my actually existing right to vote in exchange for a system of voter competency testing that has a terrible track record of abuse (as even Brennan admits) in the hopes of 'competent' government that implements policies that I, in my female, not-quite-WASPish-induced ignorance, disapprove of?

I don't think so.

Rule by the deep state (Bryan Caplan)

Like Brennan, fellow libertarian Bryan Caplan is partial to the idea of ensuring that 'correct' decisions are taken by explicitly prohibiting the incapable (as evidenced by their failure to embrace laissez-faire economics) from voting.

He floats the idea of making people pass an economic test or obtain a college degree in order to vote,[12] but his go-to strategy for the short term is to encourage his readers to '[s]ubvert bad ideas, and lend a helping hand to good ones' by exploiting the lack of oversight in their jobs at regulatory bureaus, in government advocacy groups or drafting legislation to pursue their own agenda.[13] Indeed, according to Caplan, well-placed individuals have a duty to engage in deliberately countermanding popular will (particularly on points like economic regulation), because 'the voter who acts on his biased judgement is not just hurting himself. If you employ your political wiggle room to improve policy, you are doing your part to tame public nuisance.'[14]

Unfortunately, this entitlement attitude towards invalidating democratic decisions one doesn't agree with isn't just theory. An anonymous public official penned an op-ed for the *New York Times* in late 2018 in which he claimed to be working for President Trump, and in which he assured the public that he and others were secretly 'thwarting' the President's 'more misguided impulses' on issues like trade and foreign relations, while cooperating on the ones they agreed with, like increased military spending and tax breaks. According to the (unknown and unelected) author, '[t]his isn't the work of the so-called deep state. It's the work of the steady state.'[15]

However, while people are already putting Caplan's ideas into practice, and seem to feel themselves fully authorized by their own sense of self-righteousness to subvert electoral results, Caplan himself claims that using this 'political wiggle room' to intentionally subvert public decisions works best as a two-player game, with politicians claiming to adhere to a certain policy in public while privately encouraging their subordinates to work towards different ends. As an example of this operation in action, Caplan cites the 'putatively noble' purpose of American covert support for the Nicaraguan Contras during the 1980s,[16] and, while he does not appear to necessarily support this episode of American history, he also doesn't lay out its salient details – so allow me. They are, after all, rather off-putting.

In a nutshell: in 1979, Nicaraguan dictator Anastasio Somoza was overthrown by Sandinista rebels. The United States had supported the Somoza clan for more than forty years; their opponents, the Sandinistas, took their name from a prominent rebel who had been killed by an earlier Somoza in the 1930s. Despite the fact that the Sandinistas pledged to (and in fact did) hold elections, their policies tended more to the left than to the right, so the USA covertly funded a right-wing paramilitary operation intended to violently overthrow their government. This force was none other than 'the Contras' that Caplan is referring to and the USA supplied them with military aid and advice, including – famously – a manual that outlined psychological warfare tactics intended to terrorize the population of Nicaragua, and that encouraged the murder of Sandinista officials and even of pro-Somoza colleagues in order to create 'martyrs'. Thanks to the 'steady state', American citizens didn't have to be involved in these hair-raising decisions at any point. The full truth only came out when American support for the Contras, including the aforementioned manual, became the subject of the International Court of Justice's arguably most famous case,[17] one that ended with the court finding that the USA had violated international law and ordering it to pay compensation.

Encouraging people to work from the shadows to subvert public decisions they disagree with may have sounded bad enough on the surface, but it is even scarier when you realize that Caplan is *literally arguing* to use the same strategy that helped to kill people whose major crime was wanting to get out from under a dictator and have a bit of material equality. That point remains, however much Caplan may be convinced that in his world, only truly noble purposes such as 'tak[ing money from Big Oil to oppose controls' would be pursued under this strategy.*

Ask yourself if this is really the world that you want to live in.

Plausible deniability, corruption 'for my own good'

---

* According to Caplan, this would '[turn] a private vice into a public virtue', (*Myth of the Rational Voter*, l. 3291).

and shadowy right-wing palace coups with lacings of terror and bloodshed?

I think I'll stick with democracy.

Rule by the market (Ilya Somin)

Like Caplan and Brennan, Ilya Somin views 'protectionist' economic policies as erroneous and anyone who votes for them as self-harming.[18] Unfortunately, in his view, the influence of the affluent (who are, of course, the most knowledgeable as evidenced by their lack of support for economic protections) is not quite high enough to offset the influence of the middle class and poor (who, in their benighted state, favour such protections) in the current electoral-representative system.[19]

So in order to reduce the impact of these more numerous voters, Somin proposes to limit government itself. Voters can't influence what isn't there, right?[20]

Just like if you burn down your house, no one can rob you. It's logic.

And by Somin's logic, if government is smaller and fulfils fewer functions, voters can have the same absolute amount of knowledge as they do now, but will technically be less ignorant on any given issue.[21] If your country has no public healthcare policy, for example, it is impossible for you to be ignorant of that policy.

In order to achieve this blissful state, Somin advocates that a nation's highest courts cut down on the number of laws and regulations by overturning them.[22] This, in turn, will allow the people to decide more accurately on various issues on a private one-to-one basis, because a concept that Somin refers to as 'foot voting' (that is, taking a concrete action like making a purchase or moving house),[23] gives them better incentives to make correct choices.[24] As an example, he cites that many people are against free trade as a policy, but that once foreign goods are on the shelves, people buy them.[25] Since, in Somin's view, being pro-free trade is right, this means that when people are buying non-tariffed products on the shelves, they are making a 'correct' choice, but when they band together to make a collective rule to prevent such products being on said shelves in the first place, they are making an 'incorrect' choice.

However, weirdly, people only make the choices that Somin desires once they've been manoeuvred into a position where those are also their *only* choices.

Free trade deals, for example, often force citizens to act as competitive stateless individuals unable to make common rules, such as setting tariffs to protect internal manufacturing. There's therefore no evidence to conclude that people end up at Wal-Mart because they have suddenly become convinced that giving up a pension and their children's future is a good trade-off for $3 underwear, rather than because, while there is a lot of sense making collective rules around labour rights and wages, once that is removed from your possible avenues of action, there is little sense being the only individual who is willing to pay top-dollar for their unmentionables.

Thus, while Somin claims to be a libertarian – a person in favour of maximizing freedom – like all anti-democrats, he is actually advocating *limiting* people's options to the point where the only available action left is the one he wants them to take and then claiming that the fact that people under duress behave in his desired fashion proves how sensible his views are. It's a typical anti-democrat rig.

Even more than free trade, however, Somin likes the

idea of upping stakes and moving home as the ultimate form of 'foot voting'. This could be to a different gated community (and in Somin's world you're going to need those gates), or, better yet, a different state or country altogether. A fair chunk of Somin's book *Democracy and Political Ignorance* is devoted to a lengthy argument on the alleged advantages of foot voting over ballot box voting, utilizing the example of black migration from southern to northern states in America during the Jim Crow period (1870s–1950s).[26] According to Somin, despite the fact that at the time many black people, having so recently been slaves, were uneducated and illiterate and thus would have had difficulty 'acquiring information', they were able to access 'firsthand reports from trusted friends and relatives' about conditions in the North (which could be summarized as 'more voting, less lynching') and make up their minds to move there.[27] When they started to lose too many black workers, some southern states revised some of their most repressive laws,[28] proving his point (Somin thinks) about the wonders foot voting can achieve in getting the kind of legislation you want.

Lots of things are said to be offensive these days, but this has got to be a top contender for one of the most tactless arguments ever made in favour of reducing the scope for collective action and voter impact.

As an example of the wonders of 'free choice', the one between putting up with an oppressive situation where one might be lynched and moving to a location where one might at least find a job, seems inadequate. It is also unclear how exactly black Americans who chose to leave really benefited from their home states' mitigating their behaviour after they left. But leaving all that aside,

Somin's theory also entirely misses the point that it was the very *absence* of black citizens' rights to express their preferences *at the ballot box* that allowed segregation and other forms of oppression to flourish. Had African Americans not been systematically disenfranchised, it more than stands to reason that they would have voted for policies more favourable to them, and that a lack of formal education would not have inhibited this. The only thing Somin's example illustrates is what a dangerous thing it is to be disenfranchised. It is no coincidence that lesser rates of abuse of black people correlated with their greater opportunities to vote in the northern states. Political participation, even on the thin level of casting a ballot in elections, has certainly proved to be a more efficient way of stopping flagrant mistreatment than moving house, an act of desperation that requires one to cast oneself on the mercy of whatever remaining options one has.

Somin's proposal amounts to raising the costs of each political act (moving jurisdiction) to astronomical levels while simultaneously removing citizens' ability to individually choose to collectively pass laws on issues they care about. In other words, it is explicitly designed to prevent regulation on those issues that enjoy *high levels of consensus*.

As Somin himself says, 'foot voting through international migration may be the best hope for many of the most oppressed people in the world'.[29] The question is why anyone would want to voluntarily join the 'most oppressed'.

I think I'll pass.

Fixing Politics the Anti-Democrat Way

Long live the party! (Jonathan Rauch and
Benjamin Wittes)

As I said, I started with the least palatable options.

Although free market fanatics like Brennan, Caplan and Somin are probably more of a threat than most people realize, they are generally regarded as the fringe sideshow in intellectual circles, where their choice of phrasing tends to fall outside the pale.

Germans have a perfect word for this concept (Germans have a perfect word for everything because in German you can just slam words together until you come up with the right one for the occasion). That word is *'salonfähig'*. A *salonfähig* idea is one that you can repeat to strangers at a cocktail party without them choking on their brandy. 'Isn't Picasso a divine artist?' No one is going to argue with that. *Salonfähig*. 'We should help the poor.' Well, who's going to say no? *Salonfähig*. 'Education is terrific! Of course I love children! Venice is marvellous, but oh the tourists!' ... You get the idea.

But ... 'We should subvert democracy by using our personal clout to secretly pursue our own aims within the deep state, like that time we armed those right-wing thugs to try to restore dictatorship to a tiny, impoverished nation'?

Now someone's sputtering up part of a Martini and trying to figure out whose embarrassing relative *you* are. *Not salonfähig*. Off the menu, my friend. And next time, warn people before they bite off the toothpick along with the cocktail sausage.

Thus, the truly scary bits of anti-democratic thought are not the kinds of things spouted by Somin and Caplan – although they, of course, serve as a giant tip-off as to what the ultimate anti-democrat destination is – the truly concerning parts are the *salonfähig* bits, the ones that parcel out the poison more digestibly.

Caplan and Somin (and Jason Brennan, too) might be drinking their absinthe pure, blissfully unaware that it's starting to show, but the more suave anti-democrats have the sense to stir it into some kind of festive punch and wait for it to knock your socks off when you're least expecting it.

Because that's civilized.

Salonfähig even.

And one of the most beloved *salonfähig* ideas among political pundits to combat the perils of the common person's involvement in politics is to simply batten down the hatches and return more political control to the parties themselves, primarily by increasing their say over who can be a political candidate and which policies those candidates can pursue. Democracy, in other words, must be controlled from the top for everyone's good. According to Jonathan Rauch and Benjamin Wittes, the Brookings Institute fellows who push this theory the hardest, such a harmonious state is achieved by strengthening the role of: 'state and national party committees, county party chairs, congressional subcommittees, leadership PACS, convention delegates, [and] bundlers'[30] who, despite being 'high-handed, devious, [and] secretive' have (in the past) 'brought order from chaos' by creating a tightly controlled party hierarchy, in which '[a] loyal, time-serving member of Congress could expect easy renomination, financial help, promotion through the ranks of committees and leadership jobs, and a new airport or research centre for his district. A turncoat or troublemaker, by contrast, could expect to encounter ostracism, marginalization, and difficulties with fund-raising.'[31]

Rauch and Wittes themselves refer to this situation, in which political parties explicitly seek to destroy the careers of all members who fail to conform with orders from the top brass, as 'rule by hacks'. For the spring chickens among you, that's 'hacks' not 'hackers'. A 'hack' is defined as: 'a professional who renounces or surrenders individual independence, integrity, belief, etc. in return for money or other reward in the performance of a task normally thought of as involving a strong personal commitment'.[32]

Inspiring, yes?

Surely, one would think, these two fellows of one of the most prestigious think-tanks in America are not saying that we would be better off governed by a set of people who have renounced their integrity in return for money. But it is. It is *exactly* what they are saying.

Rauch and Wittes, who routinely write in some of the nation's most illustrious magazines, also explicitly endorse elite corruption. Indeed, they reject any attempt to clamp down on 'influence-peddling', because it would prevent contributions playing their role as 'political bonding agents'. Rauch lets us know just how these bonding agents work:

> When a party raised a soft-money donation from a millionaire and used it to support a candidate's campaign (a common practice until the 2002 McCain-Feingold law banned it in federal elections), the exchange of favors tied a knot of mutual accountability that linked candidate, party, and donor together and forced each to think about the interests of the others. Such transactions may not have comported with the Platonic ideal

of democracy, but in the real world they did much to stabilize the system and discourage selfish behaviour.[33]

You may be struggling to understand how a millionaire buying politicians' loyalty qualifies as non-selfish behaviour, but the more pressing question would seem to be how people who are not millionaires participate in the 'knot of mutual accountability'. I suspect that the answer for many anti-democrats is simple: if you are not a millionaire, you aren't a person, either.

But Rauch and Wittes don't stop there. While Achen and Bartels's favourite word is 'respectable' and Daniel Bell, as we will find out, is partial to 'superior', Rauch and Wittes are in love with 'smoke-filled rooms'. In the past, as they let us know again and again, decisions were made behind closed doors in 'smoke-filled rooms' and a glorious era of carcinogenic merry-making that was. One of the smoke-filled room's chief virtues was that it allowed politicians to engage in pork barrel deals, which Rauch lets us know 'is a tool of democratic governance, not a violation of it',[34] as well as in 'candid' negotiations, which these days, unfortunately, have to be conducted in a smoke-free, open-air environment.[35] Regrettably, all this airing of dirty laundry has led people to trust politicians less. The blame for that, of course, lies squarely with 'the people', who just don't understand that this is the only way to get things done.[36]

If we lived in an era with the right of *prima noctis*,* I have little doubt that Rauch and Wittes would be

---

* Also known as 'droit de seigneur', this describes the situation where the King gets the right to sleep with every woman in the realm on her wedding night. (For the record, it is generally believed that no such rights ever actually existed, and that most kings managed to be promiscuous on a much more ad hoc basis).

defending it on grounds of being a harsh necessity, since the king is a busy man and doesn't have time to date.

Rauch and Wittes also believe that voter involvement in politics should be severely restricted. After all, voters are just too unsophisticated to cope with 'complexities, trade-offs, and specialized technical details'[37] like apparently, accepting million-dollar donations to achieve an 'accountability-bond'.

But Rauch and Wittes aren't just talking nostalgia in the abstract – they are willing to get right down to the nitty-gritty about exactly the kind of rule we can expect under the 'hacks'.

Both Rauch and Wittes, and Achen and Bartels (whose work on voter irrationality Rauch and Wittes take as a jumping off point for their own) praise the Democratic Party operatives who managed to get Hillary Clinton nominated as their presidential candidate over Bernie Sanders. Indeed, Rauch recalls the good old days, when Prescott Bush, father of George H. W. Bush and grandfather of George W. Bush, got 'started in politics' by no more complicated a method than 'a top Pan Am executive and a mover in Connecticut politics' calling him up and offering him the nomination for a seat in Congress. By contrast, in the present degenerate age, politics is full of 'usurpers' and 'insurgents who owe nothing to anybody',[38] the darkest among them being one Sanders, Bernie, whom Rauch describes as a 'political sociopath', with 'plans for governing [that] were delusional'.[39] Like anti-democrats in general, the author offers no substantiation whatsoever for the claim that Sanders's policies were delusional (indeed, most of them amounted to nothing more radical than bringing the US into line with the normal living conditions in the rest of the Western world, including, but not limited to, those enjoyed by the 36 million Canadians living right next door). He merely lets us know that such people need to be 'selected out' and that hacks would have achieved that more easily if only Americans weren't so insistent on their right to vote in primaries and would let things get back to smoke-filled room territory where these kind of political executions can be carried out in peace and quiet.[40] Considering the ultimate outcome of the 2016 American presidential election, as an example of political insiders' superior judgement in candidate selection, it's hardly a stand-out case.

But the biggest news is yet to come.

As their star example of superior professional decisions and what the future of democracy should look like in a world run by 'hacks', Rauch and Wittes offer up nothing less than the US intelligence oversight system. As the authors point out: 'The public has no access to the CIA and the NSA and their day-to-day work', which has therefore been 'resistant to populism'. According to Rauch and Wittes, although we have no way of verifying that intelligence oversight is working exceptionally well, it is working exceptionally well precisely because we don't know anything about it.

If there is one thing anti-democrats excel at, it is circular logic.

Not to be deterred by this less than promising start, Rauch and Wittes take, as their model of what democracy should aspire to be, 'the Foreign Intelligence Surveillance Act (FISA) Court'.[41]

FISA, you may be thinking, FISA. That rings a bell and it's not a good one.

No, it's not.

The FISA court is pretty much synonymous with the term 'government overreach'. And why is that? Perhaps because the FISA court, which operated at the mercy of insiders without public scrutiny, didn't stop the US's National Security Agency (NSA) from putting nearly every person in the Western world – and then some – under surveillance, while granting approval of nearly every last request to tap American citizens in the USA. Since 1979, the court has approved 40,117 warrants, while rejecting only 21 (9 of them after former NSA-contractor Edward Snowden blew the whistle on this very situation in 2013). That is an approval rate of 99.95 per cent.[42] The NSA doesn't collect three billion pieces of intelligence a month[43] by having effectual checks on its power.

Somehow, the fact that the NSA was breaching constitutional rights was not counteracted by any of the insiders who knew about it until 'the people' found out when Snowden blew the whistle. In doing so, Snowden went outside the system, which had no effective internal self-correction mechanisms, and is still living in exile, as even now, despite being almost universally acknowledged as having revealed wrongdoing, *he* would be punished if he returned to the United States.

There is hardly a worse imaginable case for oversight 'functioning' far from public view.

Running a democracy like the secret service does not make any sense at first glance, and even less at second or third glance.

But although what they are saying is stupid to the point of farce, one should not underestimate the danger that anti-democrats represent. In Rauch and Wittes's writings, one can clearly see how the groundwork laid by academics in allegedly proving the irrationality and ignorance of the masses is taken as a given in elaborating a working plan for excluding them from power. Intentionally or unintentionally, anti-democrats of various ilks work hand-in-glove to build the plan for getting rid of 'the people'.

So ... remove whole swathes of government activity from public oversight while ensuring that the in-crowd get to hand-pick policies and candidates?

I think not.

Rule of the superior (Daniel Bell)

I'm Canadian and so is Daniel Bell, so let me take this opportunity to apologize for him in advance. If you thought that Justin Bieber was the worst we had to inflict on the world, I'm afraid you were mistaken.

Admittedly, Professor Bell, in keeping with the national ethos, has been less obtrusive (more *salonfähig*, one could say) than, for example, Brennan or Caplan in his work, but he is nonetheless a passionate advocate for the (theoretically) meritocratic style of government practised in modern China, and a critic of democracy. In his book, *The China Model*, Bell wastes no time in explicitly stating that his purpose is to defend 'the idea that political power should be distributed in accordance with ability and virtue' rather than equally to just *any* passing riffraff.[44] Indeed, in Bell's view, it is paramount that power be held only by wise, moral and superior persons, selected for these attributes not by voting, but on the basis of exam scores and past performance.

Now admittedly, 'wise, moral and superior' all sound like good things and would seem to set a very high, almost fairy-tale-like bar for the aspiring politician to

94

meet. Will the successful applicant have a solid track record of vanquishing the nation's foes on the battlefield and dispensing justice to the kingdom's poor? Should they be prepared to give references on 'number of dragons slain', 'evil enchantments overcome', and 'wisdom-enhancing potions quaffed'?

In the anti-democrat world, in turns out, things are a bit more banal.

According to Bell, one already qualifies as superior, wise and moral (and thus authorized to make political decisions on behalf of others) just by possessing the ability to 'understand complex arguments', having 'a global outlook', being 'adaptable, agile and responsive to looming global risks',[45] possessing social skills and emotional intelligence[46] and being 'virtuous'.[47] In other words, what you need to be a wise, moral and superior leader of the nation is basically the same skill set required for a middle-management job at Accenture.

It's all rather anti-climactic.

But things don't stop there. Continuing the slide down the ladder, one can apparently tick the 'virtuous' box on Bell's list of qualifications just by *wanting* 'to promote the good of the people',[48] which, in turn, is synonymous merely with not being corrupt.

The 'wise, moral and superior' business isn't as hard as it looks.

However, sadly, even the low bar Bell sets for these attributes is not met in modern China, where, as Bell himself admits, corruption is widespread. And while he rather limply suggests that corruption could still be mitigated by banning public officials from playing golf with businesspeople,[49] and legalizing 'small gifts to officials' or, in Bell's words (echoing Rauch and Wittes), 'what *looks* like corrupt politics',[50] I shall go out on a limb and suggest that if a firing squad doesn't put you off corruption, I highly doubt that banning golf dates will.

Possibly aware of this shortcoming in his argument (which after all is ultimately aimed at convincing us to give up our votes in exchange for this 'meritocratic' rule), Bell tries to brazen things out by inventing a vast double standard intended to exonerate the virtuous for their flagrant lack of obviously virtuous behaviour and show that they can still count as 'wise, moral and superior' leaders.

In the service of achieving this transmutation, Bell lets us know that corruption in meritocratic China is closely entwined with low public salaries. Indeed, he tells us that, disgracefully, former Prime Minister Wen Jaibao, whose family somehow managed to accumulate a fortune of $2.7 billion, only earned the pitiful official salary of $19k a year. According to Bell, while such corruption may be regrettable, it cannot be avoided if salaries do not 'cover the basic needs of officials and their family members'.[51]

While that reasoning seems to have convinced quite a few people, over here in *On Beyond Zebra* territory, it prompted one obvious question: just where was the magic cut-off point between $19k and $2.7 billion at which Wen Jaibao's 'basic needs' were met?

Answer: probably around the 10k mark – that is, the average annual wage of an urban-dwelling person in China.[52] A salary of 19k a year, *double* what the average person in China's *urban areas* is bringing home, is also, incidentally, 4k (or about 20 per cent) higher than the annual federal minimum wage in the United States, and higher than average earnings in most of Eastern Europe.[53] Yet, in America, Poland, the Czech Republic (and one imagines in China), poor people are not habitually excused from engaging in illegal behaviour to better their finances, nor are they considered to be exceptionally virtuous when they do. Certainly no one would continue to view them as engaging in some kind of fiscal self-defence at the point where they had clocked up nearly three billion dollars' worth of assets.

Bell, however, manages, much like Rauch and Wittes did in their 'bonds of accountability' story, to transmute the 'superior' ruler's self-interest into something not only excusable, but actually praiseworthy.

It turns out that officials *need* to be lavishly compensated in order to activate their virtuousness. In 2007 in Singapore, a country that appears multiple times in Bell's book as an aspirational model, the government pegged 'the salaries of ministers and permanent secretaries to two-thirds of the median salary of the top eight earners in six professions' in order to compete for 'talent' with companies like McKinsey and Goldman Sachs. That upped the annual salary of 'entry-level ministers and senior permanent secretaries ... from $1.2 million to $1.6 million and the prime minister went from $2.5 million to 3.1 million'. Bell further lets us know that 'high potential talent' in the elite Singaporean Administrative Service can be earning $316k by the age of 32.[54] This extravagant pay serves to reduce the temptation for corruption and ensures that people are not 'penalized' for taking up a public service job.[55] In other words, Bell proposes to remove the incentive for corruption by giving 'virtuous' officials the tax dollars of ignorant voters up front.

One could, one imagines, widen the applicability of this theory and reduce the number of armed robberies by simply driving armoured vehicles up to the houses of known criminals and dumping the money on their lawns.

Under the 'rule of the best', this is what virtue looks like.

So while Bell's theory may sound tempting – the myth of the 'good king' who uses his wisdom and ability to protect his subjects in a harsh world – up close, you can't avoid seeing the tarnish on that tin crown.

But rather than accept that corruption is a noticeable fly in the ointment of Chinese meritocracy, Bell uses one last typical anti-democrat argument to excuse himself from really having to deal with it. He points out that he is merely defending 'the ideal of China, not the reality'.[56] Thus, *real* problems – like corruption, economic inequality, environmental damage, abuse of power, punishing political dissent, repression of religion, discrimination against women,[57] China's long history of exams plagued by cheating, domination by the wealthy and tests for ideological purity,[58] lack of diversity in the social backgrounds of leaders in China and Singapore[59] and the fact that political loyalty, social connections and family background play at least as big a role in political advancement in China as ability and morality[60] (all of which Bell brings up himself) – can be dismissed as not implementing meritocracy well enough.[61]

In *reality* things might not be so great, but *ideally* they would be.

Thus, we should brush aside our concerns and import 'meritocracy-lite' ASAP.

And Bell already has plans for that.

He straight up says that '[t]he uncomfortable truth is that the best (perhaps only) way to reduce the political influence of ignorant voters is to deprive them of the vote'.[62] However, he admits that such direct methods are practically infeasible, and that even a political system that divides power between an elected house of representatives and a house composed of eminent persons carefully filtered through examination for, one assumes, their 'global outlook' and hypothetical virtue,* would, unfortunately, never be accepted in a Western-style democracy[63] because '[t]he sad fact is that citizens in electoral democracies won't even question their right to choose their political leaders, no matter how intellectually incompetent or morally inconsistent their [the voters'] political judgement may be'.[64]

Western people, Bell concludes, will probably only be jolted into giving up their votes and accepting elite rule by an event causing radical change, such as major alterations to the labour and energy markets, global warming, nuclear war or a major terrorist attack.[65]

I'd pause for a moment over that thought.

So while we all await the happy day where pure fear could induce us to more willingly submit to our 'agile and responsive' overlords and their mighty abilities to 'understand complex arguments', Bell sees the future of the China model mainly in developing countries.[66]

That conviction, however, hasn't stopped him from becoming the director of the US-based Berggruen Institute's Philosophy and Culture Center.[67] The

---

* Brennan also suggests creating a similar 'Epistocratic Council', with the power to veto 'malicious, incompetent, or unreasonable', legislation or electoral results.

Berggruen Institute is an organization founded by billionaire, private investor and coauthor of the book *Intelligent Governance for the 21st Century: A Middle Way Between West and East*[68] Nicolas Berggruen, who modestly named the institute, its affiliates and prizes after himself.

Like Bell, Berggruen advocates a 'depoliticized meritocracy' to prevent 'short-term populist sentiment' from harming 'the long-term common good'.[69]

Berggruen's ideas (which remember, he and Bell aren't just talking about, but actively supporting through all his institutions and prizes) of what would harm the long-term common good are also quite similar to Bell's. Taxing the rich is a prime example. Fortunately, Berggruen and his crew are on it, and willing to work against such ill-considered plans as Prop. 30 – the California ballot initiative, mentioned earlier in this book as the measure via which California raised $6 billion by increasing tax on incomes over $250k.

As Berggruen explains:

> Governor Brown, the California Federation of Teachers, and other groups, fuelled by the 99 percent movement, sought to close the state's funding gap by taxing the easiest target – the rich. They did so because it is far more politically viable to tax 'others' than the broad middle-class that makes up most of the voting public, even though as our own Think-Long Committee recommended, a modern broad-based sales tax on services in which everyone pays slightly more would stabilize revenues for years to come.[70]

That's right, a depoliticized meritocracy would make 'objective' decisions just like billionaire Berggruen's that he is but an 'easy target' and othering-victim of taxation, which justly belongs on the shoulders of the 'broad middle-class'. Apparently, his billions must be saved under his caring stewardship so that we can tax them at some future hypothetical point, provided, I suppose, he doesn't decide to blow it all on a couple of yachts.

In order to achieve this goal and keep their well-deserved dollars safe from people who only think in terms of their own petty interests, the Berggruen Institute, which also, according to Berggruen's vision, wants to do away with direct elections to the state legislature, has already convened their aforementioned 'Think-Long Committee'. They hope to eventually transform the Committee into a permanent 'Citizens' Council for Government Accountability', a thirteen-member panel of blue-chip citizens appointed by the governor and legislature of California that will 'evaluate initiative proposals as well as place initiatives directly on the ballot on behalf of the public interest'.[71]

Other members of the Berggruen Institute include: Gerhard Schroeder (former Chancellor of Germany), Nicolas Sarkozy (former President of France), Fareed Zakaria (television host and columnist), Condoleezza Rice (former US Secretary of State), Julian Baggini (the philosopher who argued so forcefully against democracy in the *Guardian* article quoted at the beginning of this book), Guy Verhofstadt (former Prime Minister of Belgium), Mario Monti (former Prime Minister of Italy), Pierre Omidyar (billionaire and media owner), Reid Hoffman (co-founder of LinkedIn and board member of Microsoft), Niall Ferguson (political advisor and columnist), Jacques Delors (former President of the European

Commission), Jack Dorsey (CEO of Twitter), Tony Blair (former Prime Minister of the United Kingdom) and Carl Bildt (former Prime Minister of Sweden).[72]

This is not the kind of line-up that says either 'grass-roots' or 'disorganized'. So, while you may never have heard of the Think-Long Committee or Daniel Bell or any of these other strange anti-democrats before, this is all actually quite serious.

Presumably, the groundwork is in place and waiting for an opportune terrorist attack to make us realize the great benefits of 'meritocracy' and that it would be in our best long-term interests to tax ourselves and give money *to them* – the superior, the moral, the virtuous – so that they may remain virtuous.

Give up my vote for this?

Guess again.

Section 2: Sortition: The False Democrats

As we have seen, many anti-democrats would, if they had their way, prefer to prevent most people from having a say in politics by the brilliantly straightfor-ward expedient of making it impossible for them to cast an effective vote. However, because they recognize that they won't be able to achieve this goal any time soon, each anti-democrat reaches for a fall-back plan, such as encouraging their followers to thwart unwanted legislation (Caplan); pushing the model of 'meritocratic' government onto developing nations (Bell); or permit-ting corruption in the name of the public good (Rauch and Wittes). By putting these plans into motion, anti-democrats hope to eventually achieve their ultimate goal

– depriving most people of their ability to effectively participate in politics – by increments.

These numerous iterations on the same theme, yet derived from a variety of philosophical traditions, are already disquieting. Most alarming of all, however, is not where anti-democrats differ, but where they coalesce. When they are really pushed to the wall, nearly all anti-democrats, regardless of their ideology, tend to fall back on one particular plan: adopting sortition as a model of governance.[73] Sortition is, as it were, their final offer; the most palatable option for pushing the anti-democrat agenda under the deceptive guise of equality.

So what, you may be wondering, is sortition?

We'll get to that, but first let me warn you – this will take a while, because sortitionists are a many-headed hydra offering multiple variations on the same general idea.

At its most basic, the term 'sortition' means making a selection by lottery, that is, by pure chance. For example, drawing names out of a hat or winning the jackpot when those little bouncing balls come popping out of the national lotto machine. Sortitionists simply apply the lottery method of selecting 'winners' or 'decision-makers' to politics.

In a sortitionist world, legislators – somewhere between fifty and four hundred of them depending on who you ask – would be chosen at random from among all eligible voters. These citizen legislators would congregate and, advised by carefully selected experts, decide on what the law should be. These decisions could then be used for a variety of purposes: to 'advise' existing elected governments; to act as a second chamber, for example replacing the US Senate or UK House of Lords;

Category	Description	Legitimacy	Impossible to Cherry-Pick Results	Lack of Corruption	Effectivity
I	Public bodies or parliamentary subcommittees adopt the recommendations of sortition-selected bodies into their policy (preferred method of many academics and NGOS)	◑	○	◑	◕
II	Replace 2nd chamber of parliament with similarly-sized sortition chamber (potentially giving sortition chamber veto right on legislation, e.g. Askwith / van Reybrouck)	○	●	○	●
III	Replace parliament with legislation via randomly selected sortition groups (e.g. Bouricius/van Reybrouck)	○	●	○	●
IV	Create special sortition chamber to make recommendations for legislation that are put to referendum following government approval (Icelandic Constitutional Council, Irish Citizens' Assembly, Canadian Assemblies on Electoral Reform)	●	○	◑	◑
V	Create special sortition chamber to make recommendations for legislation that will be made by elected representatives	◑	○	○	◕

Fig. 3 Forms of Sortition

or to replace the existing political system entirely, with, as sortitionists like to put it, 'ordinary people' randomly selected to legislate.

Now, some forms of sortition are fairly benign, if also ineffective (Categories I and V in Figure 3), while others can be beneficial in combination with other democratic changes (particularly Category IV – which we will return to in Part III). However, they all suffer from common problems, and using sortition chambers to pass binding laws (or in the reverse version, to veto laws) is the truly problematic variation, and exactly the one that has proven so popular with the kind of outgoing anti-democrat who is capable of getting themselves column inches and TED talks. While the information in the following pages applies to all forms of sortition, it is mainly directed at this 'pure' direct legislation sortition.

Because sortitonists and I share a common inspiration – the historical example of democratic Athens – much of the information in this section will also be relevant to Part III. For this reason, it may be a little long, but for that it is thorough, and will save time later.

So, to get back to the point ...

Sortition can sound pretty good at first glance.

After all, this theory has the term 'ordinary people' in it, and it focuses on things like 'information' and 'experts'. If you didn't know, it would be hard to guess that such a progressive-sounding mechanism enjoys the support of people whose ultimate aim is to introduce 'foot voting' and 'rule by the superior'.

It is only when you dig a little deeper that it becomes apparent that sortitionist thinking is under-pinned by the same old anti-democratic ideology: that is, the conviction that there is One Right Way of doing things and the anti-democrat knows what that way is.

The only real difference is that in the sortitionist version, dissenting views are not directly explained away as a factor of near-hopeless stupidity or ignorance (as they are by libertarians like Bryan Caplan or Jason Brennan), but by the somewhat more patronizing idea that anyone who disagrees with them has failed to 'properly consider their views'.

As sortitionists see it, and they are quite open about this, under democracy as it stands, citizens all too often make 'objectively' wrong decisions, Brexit being a prime example. In their view, this *incorrect* decision only occurred because British people had failed to properly think things through in Britain's forty years of European membership, and when they did get information it was the *wrong* information. Clearly, on a society-wide level, it is just too difficult and complicated for the 'right' ideas to prevail.

Thus, for sortitionists, the answer is to shrink the size of the deliberating or decision-making body to a more manageable level where participants can be hammered by experts until they realize the error of their ways. As one sortitionist put it, 'there's a chasm between the will of the British people as expressed in their 52 per cent vote for Brexit and their *considered* will'.[74] This requires the increased use of 'citizen juries' to be 'overseen by a board of *respected* citizens', so that we can renew democracy not just to embody 'the will of the people, but the *safer*, more practical and generous notion of their considered will'.[75]

But not only is the need for sortition to 'rescue' us

just as illusory as all of the other anti-democrat claims, as a process it comes with some serious downsides for democracy.

Participation

Sortitionists often like to claim that small, randomly selected citizens' assemblies are somehow more 'participatory' than democracy is today, and that this is how government worked in ancient Athens, the birthplace of democracy. They thus attempt to invoke a powerful historical argument for the viability of legislating via sortition.

However, most of the people who advocate for pure sortition are not experts in Athenian democracy. If they were, they'd know that the Athenians did not, *at any point*, run a government under the banner of democracy whereby an infinitesimally tiny fraction of their eligible citizens were selected by lottery to make decisions binding on the total population.

This is vitally important, both to understanding democracy and realizing where sortitionists go so wrong. It is also vitally important to my own prescriptions for democracy. Therefore, since it is useful on so many fronts, we're going to take a quick crash course in Athenian democracy – the democracy that *our* democracy is allegedly based on.

Under Athenian democracy there were three major institutions:

- the *ekklesia* (legislative Assembly);
- the *boule* (an administrative body, also known as the Council of Five Hundred); and
- the courts.

In addition, there were a number of office-holders or officials. These officials were, in fact, mostly (but not completely) selected by lottery.

But they didn't hold any power.

Indeed, they held a status closer to the level of metre-maid than cabinet minister. They executed the decisions of the people – they did not, in their capacity as officials, initiate and pass laws like governments do today.

The Assembly – the body that debated and passed laws in Athens – was *not* selected by lottery. Citizens attended on a first-come, first-serve basis to debate and pass *psephismata* – the regular style of Athenian law or decree used for most decisions – or *nomoi* – the more rare quasi-constitutional level law. The only requirements for participation in Assembly, either as a voter or as someone speaking to a motion were that you were there, an Athenian adult, male and breathing.

Sortitionists confuse the Assembly with two ancillary bodies whose membership *was* selected by lottery. These were the *boule* and (in the second half of Athenian democracy) the *nomothetai*.

The *boule* (or Council of Five Hundred) was composed of five hundred randomly selected Athenians. As part of their miscellaneous duties they were charged with organizing the agenda for Assembly. However, the Council's control here was far from complete – any individual citizen could wander by and put in a proposal for the agenda, or make amendments to the *boule*'s generally vague proposals in Assembly.[76]

The *nomothetai* only came into existence in the second half of Athenian democracy, when the Athenians decided to more strictly differentiate between *psephismata* and *nomoi*. While *psephismata*, the more common

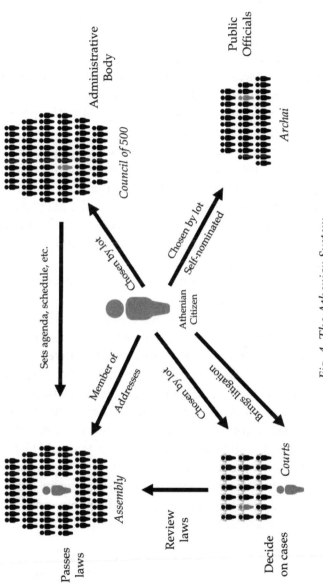

Fig. 4 The Athenian System

method of decision-making, continued to be passed just in Assembly, any new *nomos* first had to pass both the Assembly and a randomly selected panel of one thousand citizens over the age of 30 (*nomothetai*).[77] At all times, any measure passed by Assembly or Assembly and *nomothetai** could also be subjected to judicial review not by professional judges, but by 'the people' participating in great numbers.

By altering this into legislating via a small number of randomly selected citizens, pure sortitionists are confusing the administrative side-bits with the main show.

In truth, at no point in Athens were 'the people' as a whole cut out of the law-making process. There was no such thing as a law passed without any Athenian who wanted to having his say and his vote on it.

The sortitionists don't like this awkward truth, because it points up the fact that Athens was a society where the major decisions were made by what could be characterized as an endless series of referendums. It was a civilization that utilized a qualitatively different method of decision-making than that advocated by sortitionists today, and thus the success of democracy in Athens cannot prove the viability of sortitionist plans.

But this is not just because the Athenians used different methods and bodies than sortitionists would like to; it is above all the case, because unlike modern-day sortition schemes (of any sort), decision-making in Athens involved a very large percentage of the population.

Unlike the Athenians, sortitionists of all stripes, tend

---

* To be more precise, during this period the Assembly would pass a *psephisma* ordering the empanelling of the *nomothetai* for a specific purpose. However, this necessitates approval of whatever the purpose of the *nomethetai* was to be, as otherwise the vote would be in the negative.

110

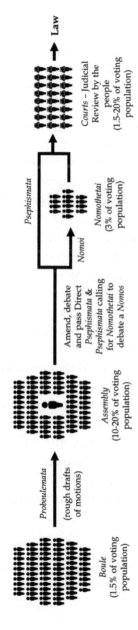

Fig. 5 Legislative Process in Later Athenian Democracy

to favour *small* numbers of citizens in their assemblies or panels, ranging from about 50 to 400. For example, Nicholas Gruen proposes the establishment of a citizens' assembly of 200–300 Britons (that would be *ca.* 0.0004 to 0.0006 per cent of the eligible voting population)* to shadow the Brexit negotiations,[78] while Askwith asks for the House of Lords to be replaced with a 400-citizen randomly selected chamber (representing a generous 0.0008 per cent of the eligible voting population). Van Reybrouck suggests that laws could eventually be made by a 400-member policy jury (again 0.0008 per cent of the eligible voting population) with an Agenda Council composed of another 150–400 people choosing topics for legislation. Prof. Robin Cohen takes a slightly different line, advocating a form of sortition that requires each randomly selected person to put in time at a lower tier of government before being randomly selected to move on to the next one. Over the course of ten years, one could eventually get up to the 500-member National Assembly (0.001 per cent of the population).[79]

The Athenians, on the other hand, were using a randomly selected body of 500 citizens just to keep track of the paperwork, and unlike Britain, which has an eligible voter population of around fifty million, Athens had about forty thousand citizen voters.

That means that Athenian democracy operated on a *massively* different scale from anything that sortitionists are advocating.

---

* As 45.7 million people are correctly registered to vote in the UK, and it is estimated that 7–8 million are not registered or incorrectly registered, I have used an estimate of 50 million eligible voters. Unfortunately, the UK does not keep statistics on the number of eligible voters, only registered ones.

Because membership on the Council of Five Hundred rotated every year and a citizen could only serve on it twice in his lifetime, about a quarter of all citizens had to sit on it at some point just to keep it functional. The Assembly was more demanding, requiring 5,000–6,000 people to turn up *every time it held a meeting*, which could be as often as every week. In addition, there were also at least 700 officials who rotated out of office on a yearly basis, and – after all that – there was still the matter of the courts. Athenian courts *were* randomly selected jury courts, but those juries were so large (ranging from 201 to 6,000 jurors) that it is estimated that each Athenian citizen had to find the time to sit on one every seven days just to make up the numbers. Such were the masses of people involved in Athenian democracy that, in an age before microphones, a strong set of lungs was recognized as a real political asset.

As these figures make crystal-clear, in Athens lotteries weren't so much a method of *selecting* people for participation (which is what sortitionists want to do) as a method for *distributing* them. That you would be selected to fulfil a particular duty in Athens was extremely hard to foresee, but that you would be selected to contribute at all was pretty much guaranteed. Political participation was *not* a privilege, it was a continual, less-than-illustrious duty that one had to share with all others. Indeed, the Pnyx Hill, where the Athenians met for Assembly, means 'squeeze tight together'.[80] As this indicates, when it came to democracy, the Athenians were prepared to place quantity over pretty much all other considerations, including comfort.

This difference in scale between modern-day sortition and Athenian democracy has enormous repercussions for the viability of both projects, as well as for our later considerations on the future of democracy – so hold on to this thought.

When we talk about ancient democracy, we speak in terms of thousands of jurors, officials and Assembly members, *because Athens was a society that could be measured in thousands.* Thus, there was an immense overlap between society as a whole and people active in government.

If we transferred the Athenian system to today's societies, we would have to speak of millions.

Transposed to modern Britain, the level of participation in Athens would have been something like:

1   Nearly 900,000 officials carrying out the orders and laws of the Assembly (twice the number of people currently employed in the British Home Civil Service),[81] plus a body of 625,000 people serving as the *boule*.
2   A quorum of at least 6.25 million people debating and passing measures in Assembly several times a month.
3   *Ca.* 1 million people serving on the courts on a daily basis.
4   1.25 million people serving as modern '*nomothetai*'.*

That is, I think we can agree, a very, very different scenario from that of fifty people stuck in a room with experts for two weekends discussing Brexit, or four hundred people serving four years in the former House of Lords.

---

*   If one chose to follow the latter rather than the earlier form of Athenian democracy.

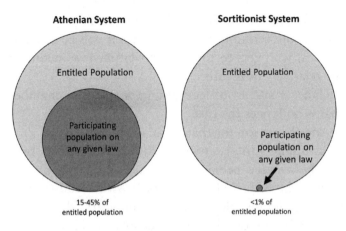

*Fig. 6 Participation in Athens vs. Participation
under Sortition*

But, you may be wondering: so what? Perhaps sortition does not reach the participatory heights of ancient democracy, but isn't it still better than what we have today?

No.

Not only is sortition less participatory than democracy in Athens was, if implemented in any meaningful way, it would also result in *less* participation by the average person than currently exists. Today, you can vote every few years, as well as try to convince your neighbours, friends and relatives to come over to your point of view – after all, they've got votes, too. It isn't 100 per cent effective, but it is still true that in our current form of democracy, people who participate more are rewarded more. There are issues with this – well-off people, for example, consistently participate more than less-affluent people – but, at the same time, there are some incentives to take part in politics and to discuss it

115

on an ongoing basis that apply across the board, because there is the certainty that every citizen will be asked to vote on who gets to form the government sometime in the relatively near future.

Under a system of legislation via sortition chamber, that is no longer the case.

And the reason for that is the numbers.

Assuming a total active citizenship of sixty-two years for the average person, if we take Askwith's plan to replace the British House of Lords with a 400-member body randomly selected every four years, that would mean 6,200 randomly selected people would serve there over the course of one's lifetime. Thus, each individual's chance of being chosen to serve in this new House of Lords at any one time is 1:125,000. Their chance of being chosen over the course of their *entire life* is 1:8,064.

Or let's take van Reybrouck's plan (borrowed from former Vermont legislator Terrill Bouricius) to institute 400-member policy juries that would be called 'whenever legislation needs to be decided on' and last one or two days.*

Between 2015 and 2017, the British Parliament passed an average of 32 Acts a year. In the USA, an average of 164 Acts of Congress were passed between 2015 and 2016, a number that includes such riveting tasks as renaming post offices (one post office at time), extending sunset clauses and making minor amendments to existing legislation.

---

* Van Reybrouck states that he would be open to such a situation in a final phase, while maintaining that a second chamber sortition body (as advocated by Askwith) is his aim for the present.

This is
you!

Fig. 7 Chance of Ever Being Chosen for a Sortition-Based 2nd Chamber

Starting with the UK and taking an assumption of thirty-two annual events requiring legislation, with four hundred people being called upon to sit on a policy jury each time, gives us a total of 12,800 participants or 0.25 per cent of the UK's fifty million eligible voters. If we spin that up over sixty-two years (thirty-two legislative decisions made by four hundred citizens each year for sixty-two years) that means that each citizen has a 15.5 per cent chance of being involved in a national decision at some point in their lives and an 84.5 per cent chance that they will *never* be involved in a national decision.

In the United States, taking an average of 164 Acts of Congress each year and assuming a four hundred-person-strong policy jury to deal with them gives us a total annual participation rate of 65,600. The USA has somewhere around 235 million voters, meaning that average annual participation rates in policy juries would be 0.027 per cent of the eligible voting population. Over sixty-two years, that gives the average American a 2 per cent chance of being involved in national legislation *once* over the course of their *entire life* and a 98 per cent chance of *never* being involved.

Moreover, many of the people who *will* be selected to be on a policy jury will get to debate and decide on nothing more important than things like the Parking Places (Variation of Charges) Act 2017 (if you are a Brit) or renaming the post office in some place you've never heard of (if you're an American).

And remember: that comes at the price of being cut out of deciding on the things you do care about.

Even the most generous forms of sortition, such as Cohen's filtration system, involve small numbers of people at the top. Cohen calls for 80,000 people to be randomly selected on to parish councils, 40,000 on to town councils, 20,000 on to borough councils, 10,000 on to county councils and 500 on to the national assembly. That means that your chances of getting into local government are about the same as always (although now divorced from your personal efforts), while seats in Parliament get reduced by 150.

When you do the math, it becomes obvious that sortition *doesn't* add more participants to the political process in any meaningful way. But it does – particularly in its final stage of replacing elected legislators – take something away. Since any person is *extremely unlikely* to be chosen to participate, and since they have *no control* over how and when they participate, their incentive to be active and informed on a continuous basis is even lower than it is now.

And that is amazing, because one of the things sortitionists pride themselves on the most is providing 'informed decision-making'.

There is, indeed, little doubt that the average Athenian (whom the sortitionists erroneously believe they are harking back to) was pretty well informed.

But why was that?

It's not because the Athenians were selecting minuscule numbers of their citizens to deliberate laws in hotel banquet halls, as sortitionists want to do. It is because massive numbers of them were front and centre speaking for motions, carrying out official duties, prosecuting court cases and casting their votes at least a couple times a week.

Every week.

Forever.

And so were all of their friends, relatives and acquaintances.

With a form of democracy that involved so many people so often, politics necessarily formed a frequent topic of conversation.

There is simply no comparison between the amount of information that can be acquired and the reflection that can occur over this constant, life-long involvement in politics, and that of even prolonged, multi-session sortition debates. No one would suggest that someone should exercise for two days straight and then not exercise for the rest of their lives. After all, thirty minutes three times a week for sixty years quickly adds up to a far greater level of lifetime total exercise. And it is precisely this steady level of democratic 'exercise' that needs to be maintained to ensure reasonably informed decision-making. Decisions, as is often pointed out, are complicated and, just like you can't build muscles overnight, you cannot build your decision-making capacity in just a few days, either. It is a continual process that involves both periods of activity and reflection.

Sortition does not provide this for the vast majority of people, and even when it does provide it – to a tiny number of people – it does so over such short, crammed periods of time as to be functionally useless. There is simply no way anyone should be making up their minds on an issue after just one or two days of debate on it. That's a barely sufficient timeframe to pick out curtains or choose a new car.

And it is quite possible that under a pure sortition system, participants would be starting discussion with a lower level of background information than most

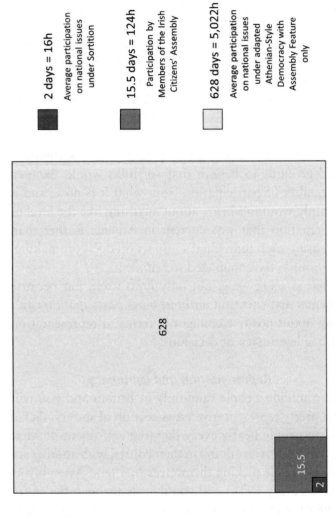

2 days = 16h
Average participation on national issues under Sortition

15.5 days = 124h
Participation by Members of the Irish Citizens' Assembly

628 days = 5,022h
Average participation on national issues under adapted Athenian-Style Democracy with Assembly Feature only

628

15.5

2

Fig 8 Average Lifetime Participation Hours

people currently possess. That is because today, people have greater incentives to acquire and retain political information than they would under sortition – after all, we do know that, at the very least, we are certainly going to get a chance to vote again.

But under sortition, the chances of being called upon to decide on an issue of national importance are extremely low, and thus the incentive to follow debates in such assemblies for anyone who hasn't been selected to participate and docs not have the means to lobby for a decision is close to zero.

So, far from offering 'participatory' benefits, there are good grounds to believe that sortition would dampen the quality of participation from what it is now, and it certainly wouldn't bring about anything like the level of participation that was current in Athens. Rather than *increasing* each individual's impact on decision-making, sortitionists have managed to *reduce* it.

That is a big issue, not only unto itself, but because it means that sortition *without mass participation* can't bring about positive changes in terms of representation and the legitimacy of decisions.

Representation and legitimacy

Pick a million people randomly in Britain and you will get a pretty representative cross-section of society. Pick a million people nearly every day (the equivalent of what the Athenians were doing in their courts, with another six million people picking themselves to attend Assembly as often as every week) and you'll cycle through the entire population in a very short space of time. Mass participation tends to automatically be quite representative.

Modern-day sortition, on the other hand, uses

sample sizes that are so small they aren't even really random. Some of the more committed sortitionists try to deny this, but during their own selection processes they control for demographics (like gender, age and ethnicity) in order to artificially make their samples representative in this regard. Picking just fifty people out of fifty million, for example, as the University College London's Constitution Unit did for a 2017 citizens' assembly on Brexit, could easily result in 60 per cent of those fifty people being men if one failed to control for gender.

If, as sortitionists themselves tacitly acknowledge – by manipulating their own selection process to hit their key performance indicators – such small numbers of randomly selected people are unlikely to accurately reflect the gender, age balance or ethnicity of society as a whole, then they are also too small to accurately represent people in any other way. Thus, small numbers of people aren't going to deliver an accurate reflection of the population's opinions, any more than they would deliver an accurate reflection of ethnic, gender or age balance without being explicitly and artificially controlled for these factors.

Some sortitionists acknowledge this issue and attempt to artificially control for political opinion. The organizers of the Brexit Assembly, for example, tried to ensure that participants were selected in approximate accordance with the percentage of the population that had voted to Leave, Remain or abstained in the actual Brexit vote. Others, however, completely fail to take this issue into consideration, and even if they were to do so, it would not be possible to control for political inclination in most cases, since few choices are as clear-cut as the Brexit vote was, nor is there necessarily always a clear and reliable record of what the general public's initial position on any given issue is.

Thus, even at the outset, the ability of small numbers of randomly selected people to accurately reflect the national political will is pretty much a non-starter.

More problematic still, however, is that, due to the small numbers involved, the impact of each participant's choice on the end outcome would be so disproportionate as to run the risk of dramatically distorting the results. This is because in a society of fifty million voters, one person's opinion is statistically meaningless* and would certainly never be used as the basis for extrapolations about general opinion. But in an assembly of fifty people who are 'representing' fifty million, one person's opinion stands in for 2 per cent of public opinion. Even in an assembly ten times as large, each person would still 'represent' 0.2 per cent of opinion. That means that in the UK each person in a citizens' assembly of 500 people would theoretically represent 100,000 other people (right now a British MP represents on average approximately 77,000 people – 23 per cent fewer).

That adds up to one important fact: small sortition bodies (of any sort) cannot accurately represent public opinion and this is particularly problematic in tight decisions. This is an issue because important political decisions are frequently taken by narrow majorities. In 1995, with 93 per cent turnout, the province of Quebec rejected a referendum to separate from the rest of Canada by 50.58 per cent (about 55,000 votes).[82] The

---

* The anti-democrats are right about that – just not in the effect that is has on human behaviour.

Irish referendum legalizing divorce in 1995 was passed by 50.3 per cent in favour (a margin of only 9,000 votes).[83] In the same country, the exclusion of suicidality as a grounds for abortion was rejected by 50.4 per cent in 2002;[84] and the abolition of the Seanad (Upper House) was rejected by 51.7 per cent in 2013.[85]

In a body of 500 people, 50 per cent (a losing vote) is 250 people, and 50.58 per cent (a winning vote) is 252.9 people. So, if two or three people acting in a citizens' assembly were to change their minds on e.g. the separation of Quebec from Canada, this would mean that two to three people would decide the fate of the nation. Even a peaceful country like Canada might have had a hard time accepting separation by a vote of two to three randomly selected people.

The legitimacy narrative of elections – that one votes for a representative who then decides for one – and referenda – where everyone has the opportunity to vote for themselves – might be flawed, but they do both provide *an anchor* for legitimacy that sortition does not: namely, that each person has the option to participate and gets a vote in some form or another.

If sortitionists aren't willing to accept a difference of approximately 1.3 million votes[86] in a referendum where everyone had the chance to cast a ballot, as they did in Brexit, as representative and legitimate,[87] then how do they expect others to accept that a citizens' assembly of fifty people, in which the vast majority of citizens were not *allowed* to participate, and in which a swing from 51.9 per cent in favour (the percentage of Leave voters in Brexit) to below 50 per cent could be achieved by *one* voter changing their minds, is right and proper?

The truth is that this only works for sortitionists,

because they view sortition as a means not of *reflecting* public opinion, but of *massaging* it to get the answers they want. Indeed, many sortitionists explicitly advocate sortition as a means of coming to *different* conclusions from those held by the population at large. For them, that a citizens' assembly would come to a different decision on Brexit from that of the majority of British citizens is not an unfortunate anomaly but the very point of the exercise.

But that's a bit of a problem when a smaller group (those selected by sortition) depends on a larger group (society as a whole) to execute or abide by its decisions.

We can see this disconnect already in the embryonic citizens' assemblies that currently exist.

Sortitionists, for example, often praise the 2015 marriage equality referendum in Ireland. In that case, a measure – legalization of same-sex marriage – that was approved by the partly randomly selected 100-member Constitutional Convention* was also approved by the population as a whole through referendum. What sortitionists often *don't* mention is that Ireland held a simultaneous second referendum, this one on lowering the eligibility age for the largely ceremonial position of president from 35 to 21. That measure was approved by the Constitutional Convention, but flopped spectacularly with the general electorate, with only 27 per cent of voters in favour. Nearly *three times* as many people voted against this second referendum as voted for it, despite the fact that it had passed the Constitutional Convention by a narrow majority.[88] Whatever the ultimate cause of the disparity between the assembly and

---

* The forerunner of the Irish Citizens' Assembly.

the populace as a whole, they were clearly on very different tracks, and this is why using sortition itself as a binding decision-making process (as suggested, for example, by Bouricius and van Reybrouck[89]) is such a recipe for disaster. There is no guarantee that the population as a whole will be swayed by the same arguments as a citizens' assembly is – and they are the ones who have to implement and abide by the decisions.

Politics is conflict mediation

Because sortitionists believe that 'every informed person' would make the same decisions they themselves would, they see the world as a place of 'right' and 'wrong' decisions rather than what it is: a place of different, overlapping and sometimes irreconcilable interests. What is good for one is not necessarily good for all.

If public transport prices go up and motor tax goes down, that's excellent news for people who drive, but not so good if you take the bus.

This has nothing to do with information asymmetries and everything to do with genuinely different interests and values. In order to settle these differences more or less successfully over the longer term, decision-making needs to be embedded in a larger informal system of negotiation and trade-offs. Decision-making is interconnected – both materially, in the sense that some decisions affect other decisions, and immaterially, in the sense that decision-making is about negotiation and 'fairness' between different genuinely conflicting interests. This is why it is impossible to snap off single issues to deal with under clinical lab conditions, and why the 'ideal' dispassionate deliberation advocated by all sortitionists (but particularly by pure sortitionists) is, at the end of the day, an artificial, sterile vacuum that may ultimately generate even *worse* conflict.

Take, for example, sortitionist David van Reybrouck's prescription for how legislating via sortition would work:

> The Policy Jury hears the various legislative proposals put together by the Review Panel, listens to a formal presentation of arguments for and against, and then votes on them in a secret ballot. So there is no further discussion, no party discipline, no group pressure, no tactical voting, no political haggling and no back-scratching ... To avoid charismatic speeches influencing the mood, the legislative proposals are presented by neutral staff members.[90]

It *sounds* good but it isn't. Group pressure, tactical voting and political haggling are harmful when they occur within a small group of people acting on everyone else's behalf and without consulting their constituents, because, due to statistical discrepancies and lack of transparency, this can exaggerate the divergence between political representation and majority will to an even greater level than elections themselves do.[91] But in real life, where those conditions do *not* obtain, these are essential conflict resolution tools.

That's why no one in any other sphere of life makes decisions in the way sortitionists advocate we should.

When you think about where you want to take a family vacation, do you make a big chart and cross everything out with equations until you get the One True Destination? I doubt it.

In real life, not only will you likely be constrained by your finances and the time you can get off work;

the current state of play in the various relationships between family members will also play a role. Did someone particularly get their way last time? Do you owe someone for giving you your way on another matter? Is having a great vacation more important to some family members than to others? What's everyone's track record on picking destinations and hotels? Are there extenuating circumstances, such as a gravely ill family member whom others wish to indulge at the expense of their own 'interests'? There are often a lot of things we need to take into account besides just 'the facts'. If your significant other doesn't enjoy sports, you're hardly going to 'inform' them into believing that their dream vacation is a cycling tour through the Alps.

Politics works the same way.

Politics isn't just about thinking – politics is about power.

And maintaining even a moderately stable balance of power requires continuous negotiation and conflict resolution, perpetual trade-offs, a constant bottom-line score sheet that has at least as much to do with perceptions of overall fairness as it does with 'objective' correctness on any one point, and a willingness to compromise, often purely because one is tired of fighting.

As long as humans are humans this is how things are going to be.

As one researcher described the Athenian Assembly:

> [T]he last thing I wish to imply is the activity of a free, disembodied rational faculty, that favourite illusion of so much political theory since the Enlightenment. Members of the Assembly were ... not free from the human condition, from habit and tradition, from the influence of

family and friends, of clans and status, of personal experiences, resentments, prejudices, values, aspirations and fears.[92]

And our societies are much more diverse than Athens was.

We need space for citizens to horse-trade over different resolutions or to complain that another group is getting their way too often and that it is time to 'share' even more than the Athenians did.

And we need to have that across the entire society. Otherwise whatever 'conflict' that led to the need for legislation in the first place will not have been 'resolved' in most people's minds, meaning that it has the potential to simply build up steam for a later explosion. Sortition, especially as advocated by pure sortitionists, does not provide *any* possibility for this conflict resolution to occur and is therefore not a recipe for success.

However, sortition doesn't just have a participation, representation and legitimacy problem; it also has a corruption problem.

Corruption

If there was one mania the Athenians could be said to have been labouring under, it lay in avoiding corruption. This was a people who rigorously examined the accounts of all public officials and who once executed nine treasurers for embezzlement over what turned out to be an unfortunate accounting error (the tenth escaped after the error was uncovered in what, one imagines, was some pretty frantic work with an abacus).[93]

Not only was the Athenian lottery system so convoluted, spontaneous and public as to be virtually impossible to crack; not only were people whisked in and out of office on strict yearly rotas: the numbers involved in decision-making *in themselves* ensured that bribery would be practically unaffordable and almost impossible to keep secret.

And even if one were to manage such a feat, its ultimate utility was dubious, because decisions in Athens could be reversed through nothing more complicated than an individual citizen starting the idea that they should be.

For all of these reasons, fixing political decisions in Athens was really hard, very dangerous and practically pointless. The incentive to make an attempt was thus minimal. Mass participation *itself* worked to discourage corruption.

At the same time, Athens provided a simple avenue for politically interested citizens to get their way – all they had to do was get up in Assembly and make a pitch for their preferred policies.

Sortitionists believe that the method we use to select politicians is the reason for their corruption, and they are not entirely wrong.[94] Electoral competition thrives on money, and that does certainly encourage corruption. However, that is only one of the main drivers for political malfeasance. The other is simply that after an election most people are excluded from exercising political power – just like they are after a sortition chamber is formed. This is an important similarity between election and sortition.

When contemplating the ills of our current form of democracy, sortitionists read the sentence, 'A small number of people, selected by election, hold power', and translate that as,

'A small number of people, <u>selected by election</u>, hold power',

putting all emphasis on the subordinate clause and identifying that as the problem with democracy and corruption in our modern age. If only people weren't selected by election!

But really, the main body of the sentence reads:

'<u>A small number of people</u>, selected by election, <u>hold power</u>'.

As long as you have a small number of people making important decisions, you'll have corruption, because corruption is economically and logistically feasible when the number of decision-makers is low *compared to the resources available in a society.*

In fact, under the system that the sortitionists have concocted, corruption would possibly be *worse* than under the current electoral system.

While anti-democrats are more than happy to castigate the majority of citizens as stupid, ignorant, fickle

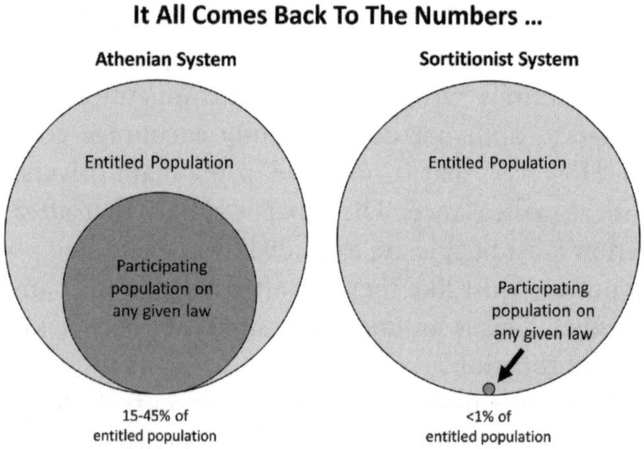

It All Comes Back To The Numbers ...

Fig. 9 Participation in Athens vs. Participation under Sortition

and racist, they don't apparently believe that they are *criminal*. Indeed, a tendency towards corruption is a quality that they – especially sortitionists – tend to attribute solely to politicians.

Thus, sortitionists often argue that because 'power has been thrust upon them', randomly selected members are not 'driven by ambition', that they have 'no incentive … to put short-term political advantage before the long-term national interest',[95] and that in a randomly selected chamber 'everyone votes according to their conscience, according to what he or she feels best serves the general interest in the long term'.[96]

Sortitionists, in other words, seem not to have noticed that the world is chock-full of 'ordinary people' who cheat on their taxes; who don't pay for parking; who give jobs to their friends and relatives, and to their friends' relatives; who patronize people they think they will get something out of; who call in sick to work when they are hungover; who return things they've used to the shop; who take credit for other people's work; who set themselves up as domestic tyrants; who keep things they 'borrowed'; who bully their work colleagues; and who put things on the expense account that technically shouldn't be there. They speed when they are late for work, tell ticket-collectors that their 14-year-old is '12 and under', buy alcohol and cigarettes for their under-age friends, give the old light-flick to let oncoming traffic know where the cops are and lend each other their public transport tickets, drivers' licences and library card. And that's just the small stuff: tonnes of people commit small thefts, acts of embezzlement, domestic abuse, vandalism, small-time drug dealing, drunk driving and assault *without ever getting caught*.

Indeed, most people's crime is petty purely because they lack ambition, imagination and, above all, opportunity.

And that is *precisely* what a sortition system would give them.

A golden opportunity to enrich themselves – and one that, as we have seen, would come just once.

While a randomly selected person may have nothing to gain politically from taking a bribe, they still have much to gain personally and – unlike politicians seeking re-election – nothing to *lose* politically. The equation in favour of corruption, in other words, is even more lop-sided than it is for politicians.

How many people might sell their vote for their own gain?

It's hard to say, but at Dublin Airport's self-serve €1 water stand, 92 per cent of people pay for the water, 8 per cent just take it[97] – and an 8 per cent corruption rate (over €1) is *a lot* to work with, as political bribery tends to involve rather larger amounts.

And that is just bribery. Among 'citizen legislators' blackmail would likely be far more effective, because – unlike politicians – 'ordinary people' haven't bargained on having their cocaine use, gambling addiction, tax evasion or love affair from ten years ago being made public or revealed to their employers and loved ones.

And on top of that there's always lobbying, another thing that politicians are used to, but ordinary people aren't. Free information conferences in exotic locations? Being buttered up by earnest young lobbyists who just want to make the world a better place?

Lobbyists don't get paid big money for being any-thing less than smart and able people, and ordinary people generally don't have a great deal of practice in a world where everyone wants something out of them and no one is their friend.

Sortitionists would no doubt respond that they would simply ban all of these perfectly possible activities, and then scream in outrage about how unfair it is when people engage in them anyway, just like they currently scream in outrage about politicians engaging in all the legal and illegal forms of corruption that it is possible for them to engage in today.

But screaming isn't going to stop anything. Even in current citizens' assemblies that *don't* generally deal with core issues, like taxation or welfare policies, activists *already* engage in distorting lobbying. Indeed, an activist once explained to an audience I was part of the tricks they had used to get access to and influence members of the Irish Citizens' Assembly. While several other people expressed horror that anyone would seek to 'corrupt the process' in this manner, it is actually perfectly natural that someone who had devoted their life to a particular cause would exploit all possible avenues to achieve their ends. The Citizens' Assembly provided them with a manageable group of people at which to aim their efforts, and it would provide that to Novartis, the Koch Brothers, Goldman Sachs and everyone else, too.

Corruption can only be effectively mitigated by curtailing both the incentive and possibilities for engaging in it – or, to put it the other way around, by eliminating motive and opportunity.

Sortition does not achieve this, because the numbers involved are too low to make corruption difficult. Instead, it relies on people being good people, but if people were completely good, government of any sort would be a waste of time.

So on all fronts – participation, representation, legitimacy and corruption – sortition without mass participation is a disaster waiting to happen.

Conclusions on sortition

Sortition isn't all bad: it is true that issue-focused debate does lead to people becoming 'more tolerant and generous towards each others' perspectives, and more liberal in outlook',[98] and that sortition can help circumvent politicians' reluctance to put difficult issues on the agenda.[99] We'll be getting back to these points in the next part and contemplating how we can use sortition constructively together with mass participation. But the key problem with sortition as advocated by most of its adherents, especially pure sortitionists, is that it fails to recognize that politics is a numbers game.

In ancient Athens, sortition was only half the story of democracy (reflective of the principle of equality) – the other half was *mass* participation (reflective of the principle of liberty). Sortitionists prefer to leave the mass participation bit out, because their preferences aren't always the same as the preferences of the masses. Instead, they prefer to work in small groups where opinion is more easily massaged over short spaces of time into what it *would be* if only people were more enlightened. In other words, under the guise of 'democracy' and 'democratic innovation', most sortitionists are actually only doing what every other anti-democrat does: trying to prevent people from doing things they don't like. Indeed, many of them hold extremely negative views of 'the masses' and their abilities to form their own political opinions and insist that the 'people' need to be carefully informed by selected 'objective' experts

136

in order to reach acceptable conclusions. According to Richard Askwith, '[t]here is ... a non-specific clamour for direct democracy that threatens to submerge representative democracy in the tyranny of the mob',[100] while van Reybrouck wants to stop 'ask[ing' everyone to vote on an issue few people understand' because '[a] cross-section of society that is informed can act more coherently than an entire society that is uninformed'.[101] Their aim, ultimately, is to control and direct rather than free majority will, particularly that majority will that they disagree with and therefore view as flawed, or, as they like to put it, 'uninformed'.

Contrary to some of its adherents' claims, sortition alone does not achieve higher levels of participation, better representation or reduce corruption. Instead, sortition significantly *cuts down* on most people's freedom to participate in politics, as it requires everyone to passively await selection to participate – for several lifetimes if necessary.

So while sortition talks a better game than Jonathan 'Corruption-Is-Good-For-You' Rauch or Bryan 'Subvert-the-State-from-Within' Caplan, on closer inspection it is the same old song. People are too stupid and ignorant to know what is good for them, so they have to be controlled, even at the expense of the equal participatory rights and mass enfranchisement that have traditionally been viewed as forming the key characteristics of modern democracy.

Far from advocating people power, sortitionists are trying hard to stem the tide *against* people power by throwing something out that appears egalitarian, but is itself controlled by a deeper layer of hierarchy (the blue-chip experts who are to 'advise' assemblies with their allegedly 'objective' information to come to 'better' conclusions than the masses would). There's a reason it continually resurfaces in the writing of so many anti-democrats.

Equality without liberty?

That's basically twentieth-century Eastern bloc communism.

Been there, done that.

Conclusions to Part II

What all anti-democrats have in common is that, rather than viewing politics as a way of mediating genuinely different values and interests, they endorse an absolutist worldview: when something is right, it is right for everyone. And since they are convinced they know what those right things are, they have no hesitations about depriving millions of people of what were up until now considered basic rights in the service of ensuring those right things get done.

In an attempt to get everyone else to go along with this, they invented some stories about how terrible people are, and then went on to invent solutions to the non-problems they identified.

They may try to give the impression of variety, but in the end, their 'solutions' to the problem of 'people' all amount to the same thing: whether it is giving up your power to the markets, giving it up to the allegedly superior, giving it up to the party or giving it up to a tiny number of randomly selected people, the main anti-democratic line is: give up.

It always has been.

But giving up political power to some other person or set of people is an unhinged fantasy that not once in human history has resulted in anything other than positively insane outcomes. Indeed, anti-democrat 'solutions' to the problem of democracy are all notable for how quickly they move from rescuing the world from bad decisions to de facto facilitating death squads (Caplan); living under the rule of secret surveillance (Rauch and Wittes); giving our money to the 'superior' bureaucrat (Bell); and depriving 99.99 per cent of all people of their vote (sortitionists).

I've called this stream of thought anti-democracy up until now for the sake of politeness, but let's call it as it is: it's thinly veiled, third-rate totalitarianism. Indeed, anti-democrats repeatedly push their ideas as a way to act 'for the good of the country', which, apparently is not necessarily the same as what most people in the country think is good for them. In other words, it's the old 'self-sacrifice for the nation' routine.

I would not advise you to give up your democratic rights for this if we were under attack by aliens and knee-deep in blood, much less for some fabricated reasons invented by bored academics.

Democracy is *not* the problem. People are *not* the problem. You are *not* the problem.

The problem, to the extent that there is one, is that we don't have real, full democracy.

And anti-democrats know this. Not only that, they know that mass, direct participation, like in Athens – real democracy, in other words – is once again, for the first time in a long time, possible.

Anti-democrats have come out of the woodwork to condemn 'the people', twist history to suit their own purposes and try to roll back rights and introduce mechanisms to lock people into rule by the righteous elite, precisely because they know very well that mass participation is now feasible, and they also know very well that, if realized, it would cut them as gatekeepers out of power irrevocably.

In other words, while some of the content of the next part of this book – on how to bring about mass participatory democracy *right now* – may come as a surprise to some readers, I highly doubt it will come as a surprise to anti-democrats.

Part III

A World You Might Want to Actually Live In (Fuller Democracy)*

I may be critical of anti-democrats for obvious reasons, but there *are* problems with democracy as we know it: due to the small number of seats available, elections aren't actually representative; money helps to win seats, which creates an entrenched relationship between wealth and power; the winner-takes-all-methodology fuels competition, leading to a consolidation of factions that become increasingly violent in their quest to achieve and retain power; an extreme form of individualism in which no one takes the common interest upon themselves comes to predominate, leading to gross inequality and erosion of the (previously successful) economic basis of the civilization; and short-term policy-making focused on the electoral cycle gradually replaces sustainable planning. All other aspects of life – religion, education, media, charity – become sucked into this vortex of conflict, as everything becomes just another tool for 'winning'

---

* Having tried and failed to come up with a snappy title for my model for years, I'm taking a page out of Berggruen's book and just christening it after my (rather fortunately named) self.

141

political power. Indeed, the extreme partisanship of many 'advanced democracies' is not an anomaly, but their natural end-state.

I detailed these self-destructive aspects of electoral-representative politics in a previous book,[1] which was significantly *more* critical of our present political system than most anti-democrats are.

However, the problems with democracy are not inherent in *the people*, as the anti-democrats claim, but inherent in *the system*. And that is extremely good news, because if *people* were the problem with our democracy, we'd really be up a creek. Humans are, after all, all we have to work with here.

In this part of the book, I'll explain what a future democracy that has people in the driver's seat could look like. In doing so, I look at what essential attributes such a democracy would need to have in order to flourish and how we can bring about change while still keeping our commitment to one-person, one-vote political equality.

However, before we begin, let me say a few words to explain the direction that my considerations will take. Unlike many pundits, my goal is not to make the world 'good' in some general fashion. Indeed, I believe that concepts like 'good' and 'evil' are theological, rather than political, matters. Also, unlike many other commenters, I come from a legal background. In the legal world we generally ascribe to a concept known as 'positive law' – namely, law is law as codified and enforced by authority. It does not matter if you, I or anyone else believes that the law is morally right or wrong, it is still the law, and a judge, for example, has a duty to apply that law whether or not they agree with it.

That may sound harsh, but this is the doctrine in which all legal professionals are trained. And why is this the case? It is because the alternative would be far worse.

In fact, not to put too fine a point upon it, there is so much disagreement on what the law *should be*, that if everyone acted on their own inclinations, chaos would reign and the rule of law, and likely civilization as we know it, would collapse. There is, on the other hand, significantly less disagreement on what the law *is*, as well as what the processes are for determining this and trying to change it, and this brings order to the world.

Thus, in my view, democracy at bottom, is not about determining 'right' laws or 'wrong' laws, especially not in some absolutist sense that is to remain valid for all time. Democracy is about determining *the law* in a manner that is egalitarian, but not necessarily always 'right' in a theological sense.

Democracy simply means 'people power'. That's it.

As this indicates, my goal here is not to lay the groundwork for a 'utopia', but merely to offer a solution to an urgent problem.

That problem is that under representative democracy as we practise it, corruption in politics leads to increasing oligarchy.

We now live in a world where highly paid executives can earn nearly a thousand times the wage of average workers *at their own companies*, where public infrastructure is being thoroughly dismantled, where billions of dollars are lost to tax havens each year and cartels and monopolistic business practices have become the norm. These developments have become such daily news[2] that they need no further explanation.

143

A World You Might Want to Actually Live In

The reason inequality has increased despite majority opposition is that elections, while certainly preferable to many other systems, have one massive flaw – they inevitably create a system where power, *however slight*, can be used to create wealth, which can be used to create power, which can be used to create wealth, which can be used to create power. In other words, elections help to create a class of people who possess both wealth and political power – oligarchs. Their virtue is to do so gradually, but unfortunately this very creeping nature often makes the problem difficult to perceive. This process of wealth and power hoarding can occasionally be reset, but it always restarts itself, and change that counteracts this process is often extremely difficult to achieve and arrives decades late.

This is the sole problem the following proposals are directed at changing – the excessive lag and interference between popular will and decision-making which tend to lead to so many decisions being taken in minority interests, a process that inevitably enriches the (ever-dwindling) minority at the expense of the majority.

Successfully applying these proposals will not necessarily result in people dancing in the streets, estranged families reuniting, or dollar bills raining from the sky, but it will get rid of oligarchical control of politics and make it *possible* to easily and efficiently make decisions according to majority will. It is highly *likely* that such decisions will then be more in the majority interest than our current system allows for, because the incentives for the majority to act in its own interests are exponentially higher than the incentives for a small, oligarchical class to do so.

A World You Might Want to Actually Live In

It is this challenging yet clearly defined problem that informs my proposed solution, which is to implement an adapted version of Athenian democracy today. There is one thing about Athenian democracy that no one disputes – it was a state where popular will ruled.

However, Rome wasn't built in a day and neither was democratic Athens. Indeed, it took about one hundred years for Athens to go from being a deteriorating aristocracy suffering a mortgage crisis to what is widely regarded as peak democracy.

Change management, especially on a society-wide level, is rarely as easy as it sounds, and this also informs my approach in this chapter.

Easy answers that promise immediate results with little effort have not been just a staple of the diet industry – they've been fairly common in the political punditry business, too. You've likely read many a long and interesting analysis that ends by pointing out a few obvious solutions to the world's problems that already enjoy near universal approval.

'Get money out of politics!', for example, is a favourite and it sounds appealingly simple. And if thirty years and three thousand books later money is still in politics, that can hardly be blamed on the authors of those books, right? They told you what to do.

But the reason the changes they like to prescribe are never likely to occur is that they focus on how things *should be* and how they *would be*, but not how they *are* and how they are *likely* to be. Ultimately, nearly all these commenters want to produce a *different result* while continuing to use the *same system*. But this system will not get money out of politics any more than an orange tree will grow candy floss. After all, it is this

145

system that put money into politics *in the first place*, because it incentivizes it and thrives on it.

If you really want change, it is necessary to recalibrate the entire system in order to incentivize different behaviour (in our case, giving people control of politics). That means removing obstacles in the way of that goal and strengthening points that support it. It's that simple.

So, rather than throwing ourselves at apparently easy, but ultimately futile, changes (like trying to 'get money out of politics', something that even if achieved on paper could be easily reversed or subverted), we are concerned here with making very difficult but deep changes, ones that do not merely seek to regulate how people *should* behave, but incentivize them to willingly behave in different patterns *of their own accord* – something that is, ultimately, far less work.

It would be nice to dramatically announce at this point that where we are going there are no maps, but actually my entire point is that we have a fairly good blueprint from Athens. However, it is also a fairly old blueprint, and because every change would *actually be a change*, we'd need to take a break after every major step, get used to new practices and reassess the situation. Real life is not a petri dish and there is little to be gained by attempting to apply some 'great theory' in exact detail. This is why, like the system of democracy itself, it is important to leave some flexibility in any plan to get there.

Thus, instead of going into great detail, I'm going to focus on five major principles. If I can implement just the first principle in my lifetime, that will already represent era-defining change, but I will include the other four here for the sake of being complete.

So ... to begin!

A World You Might Want to Actually Live In

Five Principles for Transformational (but Responsible) People Power

1   Shift to online and en masse

When we analysed sortition in the previous chapter we saw that only mass participation works as a substantial counter to political corruption – a problem that our society genuinely suffers from. This is because when the number of decision-makers is small compared to the total number of citizens, it becomes relatively easy to manipulate the decision-making process, since the number of variables one needs to control is manageable compared to the resources available. The more people participate, the harder it is both to keep secrets and to control the decision-making process. Therefore, the first, and central, challenging issue to creating a modern democracy (that is, a 'people power' state, as opposed to an oligarchy) is to ask: how can we achieve mass participation in decision-making?

As the saying is: one door closes, another opens. With each passing year, our society is becoming *less* like the late-Enlightenment group of states that introduced modern electoral politics, and more like Athens in its essential attributes. In fact, the conditions that we live under are increasingly *incompatible* with the idea of electing a small number of politicians once every four years and *more compatible* with continuous mass participation.

For the first time in modern history, it is possible for 'ordinary people' to be in constant communication with each other and thus to share knowledge quickly; it is possible to instantly record millions of votes; it is possible to know what large numbers of people want at any given time within a very short space of time; and it is possible, perhaps even necessary, to work more collaboratively, since the exponential increase in data means that while the total level of expertise is higher, it is also more fragmented than in previous decades. Perhaps most importantly of all, the prohibitively high costs of large-scale participation have sunk dramatically, making a previously unthinkable level of mass participation not just possible, but possible at bargain rates.

When scholars suggested in 2004 that a large percentage of the American population be brought together in groups of 500 voters to listen to presentations from politicians and deliberate issues over the course of a day prior to presidential elections, it was estimated that facilities alone would cost somewhere between one and two *billion* dollars.[3] That was the price tag for eight hours' worth of deliberation that would consist of nothing more exciting than using a public holiday to take a school bus to the local school and formulate questions to ask party functionaries in the gym.

People are now sharing more information than this on a voluntary basis on social media *all the time* and software already exists that can channel this information into constructive deliberation and decision-making.

In other words, for the first time, affordable infrastructure exists that would allow citizens in large nation-states to participate in decision-making at approximately the same rate as they did in Athens.

Ethelo, for example, is a Canadian-developed software providing a highly-integrated platform that allows participants to make complex policy trade-offs, indicate preferences on a sliding scale rather than a yes/no binary and provide links to external information for other participants to consider. Those taking part can also weight each factor in a decision according to its importance to them (for example, 'reducing pollution' may be more important than 'economic growth', or 'investing in infrastructure' may be more important than 'education'). This allows voters to have a greater impact on the issues that they care most about by agreeing to cede some of their voting power to others on issues they feel less strongly about. That in turn provides a far more precise idea of what citizens want and helps to evade unnecessary conflict. Rather than becoming completely polarized over a choice between A or B, citizens can possibly agree in large majorities to several aspects of both platforms while isolating only the specific points they still strongly disagree on for later discussion or inaction. Issue-specific voting also means that it is possible for voters to easily distinguish different aspects of a decision, but also to consider them as interdependent possibilities. This is a distinct advantage compared to present methods, which require voters to either endorse a party platform wholesale or to vote a straight yes or no on referenda that are themselves multifaceted and could benefit from being broken down into fewer constituent parts (Brexit would be a prime example).

Ethelo also allows voters to log on repeatedly to follow the conversation and change their votes – in other words, allowing the time for investigation and review that the researchers cited in Part I found so beneficial when testing citizen knowledge.

The most significant aspect of the platform, however, is that voters can also instantly see how the population

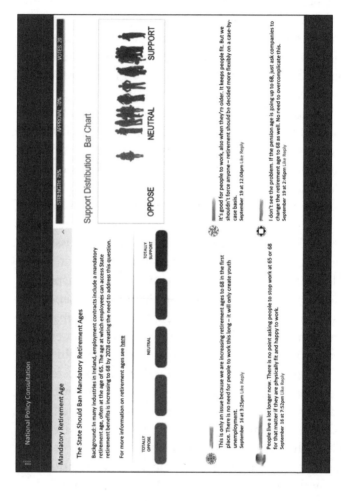

Fig. 10 Ethelo Decisions

as a whole is voting. In other words, there is complete transparency, which minimizes the need for results to be interpreted by officials (and thereby possibly skewed).

This can have negatives, such as group pressure, but it can have positives, too. After all, it is more effective to mount a campaign to try to change people's minds on a certain issue before voting ends, rather than simply cast a minority vote. That means that conflicts that could otherwise take several referenda or even electoral cycles to resolve can be dealt with more expediently, as there is no need to wait for voting results and then regroup for Round 2, 3 or 20 of a contentious discussion.

It would be simple to use this software to run anything from typical 'headline' referenda – for example, 'Should Britain leave the European Union?'; 'Should the prohibition on abortion be struck from the Irish Constitution?'; 'Do you accept the peace deal between the Government of Colombia and FARC?' – to more detailed open-ended decisions – for example, 'How should healthcare be reformed?' – to complex multidimensional local planning – for example, 'The new community centre should include a basketball court/library/gymnastic equipment', etc.

Anyone can participate in this discussion or make suggestions for new options to be debated.

This means that a process that would have once taken a huge amount of effort to organize via community meetings (that would never have accurately captured so much data) is now cheap, easy and transparent. In fact, it is significantly *easier* for participants to access information over one central hub focused on debating a specific decision than it is in the current political process that tends to revolve around endless repetitive talking points and rather sparsely scattered statistics.

Ethelo runs at about 15 cents per head of population for a month's worth of service. For a country of 235 million voters (the voting population of the USA), that is $26 million for a month of deliberation (even supposing there would be no national discount and the participation rate runs at 100 per cent). So one would pay less than 1/60th the cost of an offline deliberation day for thirty times as much deliberation, making it two thousand times more cost-effective than mass deliberation exercises conceived of only fifteen years ago.

And that's only one platform that is currently in use. There are plenty more out there.

Wisconsin-based PolCo lets people decide on individual questions, for example, 'should coffee shops be allowed to apply for liquor licences?'. PolCo allows people to vote yes or no and to comment either for or against the proposal. The software is already being used at local level and by news outlets in the United States. When I asked PolCo's CEO Nick Mastronardi to give me an estimate for a nationwide poll, he told me that the fixed costs of PolCo, down to building the platform and hiring staff, were 'a couple of million', and that a nationwide poll would cost about $20k to run with an additional $25k marketing budget to raise awareness and attract participants. Once a user base is established, the marketing costs also fall away, leaving operating costs of approximately $20k per question. In other words, national polls with a deliberative component can be conducted over PolCo for about 1 cent per 100 head of population.

Not having to assign people to physical venues,

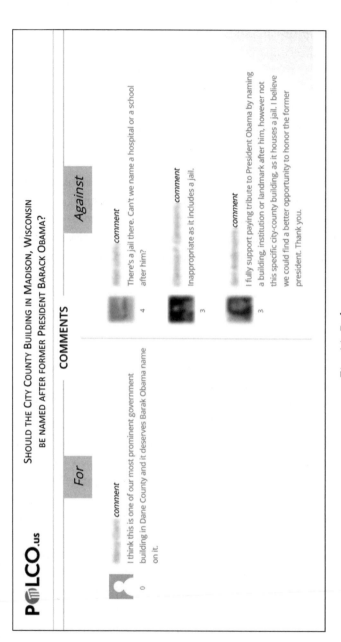

Fig. 11 Polco.us

provide on-site staff and security or arrange for facilities, catering and insurance[4] adds up to some serious savings, meaning that there is no longer any need to limit participation to small numbers of people or short spans of time. These constraints, which have been with us for so long and which have determined the parameters of political engagement, just ceased to exist.

Therefore, it should come as no surprise that there are now dozens of online participatory platforms, each with slightly different areas of focus, slightly different strengths and weaknesses, but all viable and functioning for a fraction of the costs incurred in traditional face-to-face decision-making. While some will no doubt fail due to mismanagement or an inability to attract followers, the proof-of-concept is there and it is there to stay. Indeed, the shift to mass participation is already beginning to happen almost of its own accord as a natural evolution of the political process.

In Europe, both the Pirate Party and the Five-Star-Movement already use software to formulate policy from the bottom-up and they are hardly fringe: the Five-Star-Movement won the most votes of any single party in the 2018 Italian election, while the Pirate Party is the third most popular in Iceland and the Czech Republic. The British Labour Party – now the biggest party in Europe in terms of membership – plans to test similar mass participatory initiatives in its councils, as well as to create a publicly operated social media channel to facilitate direct decision-making.[5] Similar initiatives are under way in Australia, the USA, Argentina and Ireland.

Even governments are already working towards this end, as they attempt to use participatory measures to achieve their own goals. The recent referenda on Brexit in Britain and abortion in Ireland are examples of a party system seeking to outsource thorny issues to the populace while retaining supremacy in other areas.

This has been complemented by a particular form of mass decision-making known as participatory budgeting, which has spread around the world over the past three decades. Participatory budgeting allows voters to decide directly on which projects some (or all) of the public budget is spent. This can be done via online or offline participation, or through a combination of both, as is the case in Lisbon and Dublin. Some of the more prominent examples of participatory budgeting in action include Reykjavik, which has been running participatory budgeting for nearly a decade via Citizens' Foundation; Paris, where the annual participatory budgeting exercise attracts more than 150,000 votes and disburses more than €100 million; and Portugal, which conducted the first national participatory budget in 2017.[6]

While it has also been implemented in Boston, New York and a host of British and German municipalities, participatory budgeting has been even more widely used in Latin America, where it has its modern origins. In the late 1980s, a large-scale participatory budgeting project was launched (offline) in the city of Porto Alegre, Brazil, and proved successful in several interesting ways. First, it was notable for the fact that lower-income people tended to be the most involved in participatory budgeting, and that women and young people also participated to an unusual degree[7] – all demographics that are typically underrepresented in conventional electoral political systems. But perhaps these typically marginalized sectors of society were encouraged by the fact that participatory budgeting in Porto Alegre was really

Fig. 12 *Participatory Budgeting in Iceland. Courtesy of Citizens Foundation Iceland.*

getting things done: '[P]rimary health care was set up in the living areas of the poor, the number of schools and nursery schools was extended, a lot of streets in the slums have been asphalted and most households now have access to water supply and sanitation.'[8] In addition, by its very nature, participatory budgeting tended to have a suppressing effect on clientelism and corruption.[9] When communities use participatory budgeting (and other forms of mass decision-making), it is much harder for politicians to promise goods or services to a certain segment of voters in exchange for their votes (a practice common to all electoral democracies, including Western ones), because they are simply not in a position to keep those promises. It is also difficult to hand out inflated contracts for vanity projects (the swimming pool that really didn't need renovation; the new road that doesn't go anywhere useful) if no one votes for those projects through participatory budgeting. Thus, rather than exhort politicians to behave morally or seek to find and punish those who do not, participatory budgeting does something far more effective – it limits the opportunity to engage in corruption in the first place.

While participatory budgeting and other direct democratic methods are sometimes appropriated, cancelled or reduced to window dressing, the general trend is still positive, and it is by scaling these already-tested and technologically viable concepts that we will relatively quickly get to a real democracy of mass participation.

As all of this indicates, the shift to mass participation is not something that is *about* to happen, it is something that has already started and which is becoming increasingly feasible by the hour – hence the anti-democrats' panic.

Implementing mass participatory democracy is not – unlike so many causes – a struggle *against* the natural course of progress, or a quixotic attempt to do right in the face of overwhelming odds. Quite the opposite. It merely amounts to facilitating the natural flow of history by utilizing new technologies to more fully achieve the values (majority rule, accountable decision-making, political equality) that we have been officially striving for since the Enlightenment.

It is no longer true that the huge numbers of voters in modern nation-states (or even the world) present a barrier to achieving these goals.

However, what is most important about facilitating mass participation in decision-making – something that is now both feasible and affordable – is that it virtually eliminates the scope for lengthy unresolved discrepancies to exist between majority will and actual political decision-making. It is this exact gap, which causes us so much difficulty, that is closed – and closed in a manner (deliberation, weighted voting) that actually improves the accuracy of the process.

What we need to do is constructively accelerate this process and embed it in our system of government rather than seek to destroy it, and there are three main ways to do this: increase the frequency of referenda; elect representatives who commit to voting in accordance with their constituents' votes in online decision-making platforms; and expand the use of participatory budgeting in terms of scale and value. In doing so we would scale up to an Athenian level of participation – at least in regards to the kind of decisions that were made in Assembly.

Now, an ill-considered but perennial objection to this objective is that this kind of participatory democracy was only possible in Athens because the Athenians held slaves. This enabled them to loll about eating grapes and discussing politics, whereas the average modern person simply does not enjoy that kind of leisure.

There are several problems with this argument. First, the level of political participation was much higher in Athens than anything I have suggested thus far. This is partly because I am (thus far) only suggesting changes to the law-making process, whereas Athenian citizens participated as officials and jurors as well. Indeed, participation in the courts was probably the most time-consuming obligation that Athenians had – and we aren't even touching on that aspect in this book. Furthermore, ancient peoples had to walk or at best ride a donkey everywhere they went and complete all tasks from vote counting to communicating news in manual, extremely labour-intensive ways. For these reasons, it would be quite difficult for us to sink as much effort into democracy as the Athenians did *if we tried*.

Second, Athenian men generally *did* have day jobs, and not always terribly glamourous ones, either. According to ancient writers, Assembly was attended by working people such as fullers, cobblers, smiths, farmers and builders.[10] In addition to this, Athenian men had to be fit enough and trained enough to function in the army. There *were* poor people in Athens (indeed, Athenian citizens were organized into four rough social classes, rather than one affluent class), and even some state welfare for those who could not work. Thus, it is important not to extrapolate an idea of average living conditions from the lives of the 'extremely' leisured elite, who, of course, left most of the records behind them (just as they do today). Many citizens were more in the habit of making shoes than attending symposia or writing philosophical treatises on a full-time basis. The total level of leisure that democracy required to function was thus not as high as people sometimes perceive it to have been.

For these two reasons, the Athenians were doing more with less than people generally assume.

And we would likely have to do less yet.

In Athenian times, while a significant body of legislative work had been laid down at the beginning of the pre-democratic period, life was still rather unstable. In particular, a substantial amount of decision-making revolved around war and the preparations for war, which always required new assessments.

Like us, the Athenians rarely changed their *basic* societal values. And it is due to that stability, and the kind of external stability that Athens definitely did not enjoy, that most modern legislatures really only pass about three or four pieces of major legislation a year. Legal changes generally occur very slowly and often revolve around the much easier job of amending existing laws rather than creating completely new ones. Even then, the minutiae of such tasks can be easily delegated. It would be extremely efficient, for example, for a mass decision-making body to pass a resolution that a law be written (or more likely altered) with a certain content, and for a crew of lawyers to get this done between one meeting and the next where the legislation is then passed.

So, while democracy is a lot of work, it was still well short of a full-time job in Athens and would be even less work today. In a direct digital democracy, the average person would perhaps participate in decision-making in a structured way for two or three hours every few weeks. And to be perfectly frank – there would be little point to purchasing a slave in order to free you up for two or three hours every few weeks. Even if you got a slave *for free*, it would cost you more to feed, clothe and house them than this would be worth.

As this indicates, in the ancient world, slave labour was underpinning *a lot more than democracy*.

Perhaps this is why so many civilizations that were not democracies had slaves. Be it the Romans, Egyptians, Chinese, Huns, Celts or Israelites, the major societies of the time practised slavery. In pre-colonial Nigeria, the Igbo practised a decentralized form of governance that was essentially proto-democratic in nature. Like the Athenians, the Igbos held slaves, as did neighbouring peoples who did not practise democracy. Slavery increased exponentially during the Roman Republic, so much so that it caused an unemployment problem among free Romans – yet Rome never became a democracy. And neither Sparta nor Egypt became democracies, despite holding slaves and helots (a kind of Spartan serf whom the Spartans treated significantly worse than the Athenians treated their actual slaves).

There seems, in short, to be no particular connection between democracy and slavery, but a rather obvious connection between high levels of warfare (the typical method of slave acquisition), coupled with rather strict understandings of tribal or national loyalty that made it difficult to switch citizenship. In this ruthless world, after one vanquished another people, there were often only two obvious options for dealing with survivors: kill them or enslave them.

So it wasn't so much that the Athenians (or anyone else for that matter) decided to be particularly mean to slaves by excluding them from politics – after all, chances were that either they or some other people had already destroyed their nation and slaughtered their family members, or the person in question had been unfortunate enough to be kidnapped by pirates and sold (which is really the same principle in operation).

Compared to all that, voting rights weren't really in it.

The understanding was more that clearly government (of any kind) was for the members of the tribe. Democracy, after all, was not just a fun debating club, but a deadly serious method of deciding what your 'people' were going to do on serious issues. No foreigner, including slaves, could be a member of that tribe or have the same kind of stake in its welfare (indeed, in some cases their interests would have been the polar opposite), so it seemed perfectly natural not to consult them.

So considering the ruthless world they lived in, we have to ask ourselves how an Athenian commitment to not holding slaves would have manifested itself. One would think that if the Athenians were to have believed that holding slaves was immoral, then they also would have had to believe that war was immoral, because presumably if vanquishing people and making them slaves was bad, then vanquishing people and just killing them would be even worse, and killing the men and leaving the women and children to fend for themselves wouldn't necessarily have been much kinder. Furthermore, had they refused to take slaves, this would likely have had a negative impact on their military and economic capabilities (compared to where they were with slave labour). So if the Athenians were to have held such a set of beliefs at the time, it's possible that we wouldn't be hearing about them at all, as it would have meant handicapping themselves in several ways compared to other states, none of which was really in the habit of peaceful coexistence.

Now, as you may have noticed, and I think this is really important, we live under very different conditions today, which is why this entire way of life doesn't really apply anymore. We don't share Athenian views on war or citizenship. We also don't share their reliance on manual labour that made slaves such an attractive proposition.

Had the Athenians possessed cars, dishwashers, factory robots, vacuum cleaners, toasters, microwaves, tractors, mass-produced food and clothing, gas-fired boilers, and a method of voting from home at the click of a button, there is little doubt in my mind that they would have managed democracy just fine without needing a slave around to watch the laundry spin in their washing machine for them.

Thus the question, 'Do you need slaves to create enough leisure in order to have participatory democracy?' is, in an age of mechanization, like asking, 'How many monks to you need to provide medical care to a town?' or 'How many grappling hooks does it take to effectively storm an average sized castle?'.

The Athenians could have used their slaves just to work harder and try to have more (lots of other people did), and we, living a lifestyle far above their own, could choose to do the same with our automated 'slaves'. But the problem with that is that if you don't have democracy, the economic surplus from all that work accrues disproportionately to the top layers of society (indeed, we experience precisely this issue with our modern 'mechanized' slaves). This is why you cannot work yourself into being a democracy – not now, and not in Athens, either. The central issue is not the total amount of work being done (which in our society is exponentially higher than it was in Athens), but rather the distribution of the gains of productivity.

So, to sum up: slavery (which incidentally was a rather different institution back then) was embedded in ancient times through a variety of different factors, including warfare, more rigid conceptions of identity and the need for manual labour. Societies at the time used slaves to increase their military and economic clout, but few became democracies. So while slavery certainly helped to maintain the standard of living in Athens, it also helped to maintain the standard of living in Rome and in many other cultures. Slavery, at the time, was, like war, basically a given of life, and since Athens did not exist in a vacuum, we cannot predict the effects of removing slavery from Athens without removing it from all of its competitors as well, at which point we are no longer contemplating actual history, but a parallel universe where anything is possible.

What is certain is that we don't live under the conditions that made slavery such a universal institution in ancient times, and we also don't need it to provide ourselves with a standard of living and level of leisure that is more than adequate for our purposes.

Cultural conditions have changed *profoundly* since Athenian times (and not just in regards to slavery) – it's just the underlying maths of democracy that hasn't, which is why you don't need to hold a slave to practise democracy any more than you need to hold a slave to use the Pythagorean Theorem.

2 Pay-for-participation

While there is no need to practise slavery to have democracy, it *is* important to try to support people who are time-poor to participate.

Athenian citizens received a moderate day-rate each time they attended Assembly or the courts, or carried out the official duties they had been assigned.[11] How much they received depended on a variety of factors, but it was enough to help cover the bills – perhaps the modern equivalent of $50–$100 or so.* This not only helped to keep Athenian participation numbers high, day-in and day-out, it had a positive impact on the diversity of people who were able to participate. Even ancient commenters considered pay to be a major factor in enabling people from lower socioeconomic backgrounds to attend Assembly.[12]

This is important, because in our societies today, the more affluent a person is, the more they tend to participate in politics. For this reason, and the fact that modest compensation would not be particularly motivating for them, pay is unlikely to affect their participation levels very much. But for a person of fewer means, such sums make a bigger absolute impact on their budget and are therefore far more appealing. Thus, pay-for-participation *should* contribute to evening up participation between the more and the less affluent, by providing a powerful incentive to the less well-off to participate, while giving nothing of great interest to the wealthy.

The goal being pursued here is *not* the creation of equality of outcome in regards to participation (as sortitionists

---

* Due to several factors, an exact comparison to modern day currency is difficult.

aim to do – while actually creating a deep inequality between those few who are selected to participate in sortition chambers and everyone else). The objective of pay-for-participation is merely to create realistic equality of opportunity in regards to participation (rather than a purely theoretical equality). This is because democracy rests not just on enablement, but also on accountability. While there is every reason to try to enable people who would otherwise face harsh barriers to participate, there is no reason why people who are apathetic, lazy or uninterested should be forcefully included in decision-making. In practice, this means that participation may skew towards the more educated (and then again it may not), but it will definitely skew to the more interested.

This is advantageous for several reasons: people interested in a particular topic are often more informed about it than those who are not; the interested are the people whose approval of any decision is most necessary for implementation to succeed; and participation should always be something of an effort, because it is precisely this effort that incentivizes people to want to get it over with efficiently rather than squabble eternally. For these reasons, the choice to participate must ultimately rest with the individual.

There are two (contradictory) objections to this concept of political participation as something that is financially supported but ultimately voluntary.

The first is the idea that any political system should procure a participation rate of as close to 100 per cent as possible, and that any level of unfairness between those who have more leisure or confidence to participate and those who do not must be *completely* eradicated in order to make any project of reform worthwhile. Pay for voluntary participation does not completely achieve this, but merely ameliorates inequalities.

However, this is a faulty premise because it doesn't take our dire starting position as regards participation into account. At the moment, direct participation in national decision-making in Western societies often involves around 0.001 per cent of the population. A participation rate of 0.1 per cent in national decision-making would thus already represent an increase in participation of one hundred times. A 10 per cent participation rate would represent an increase of ten thousand times.

Now, initially, it is more likely that digital participation will be mediated by political parties and elected representatives anyway, as we have seen with some of the developments mentioned above. Thus, it would be likely to begin in certain constituent areas that would serve as pockets for later expansion rather than starting out as a national project from scratch.

But let's imagine, for the sake of argument, that we did start from scratch on a national level, that we replaced elections with digital democracy overnight and that this change did not come about via popular revolution or any other mechanism that would lend itself to generating higher initial participation numbers. In fact, let us imagine that no one has heard about digital decision-making at all, and therefore in the first year of digital democracy only 1 per cent of the population participates. Let's further assume that many of these participants come from typically politically active, time-rich segments of society: retirees, students or people who were always particularly politically interested.

Notwithstanding all these problems: that is still a one-thousand-fold increase in participation.

That is an enormous difference and it is almost impossible to imagine that this would have no repercussions on the content of decisions.

Some retirees, for example, are rich, some are poor, some are in good health, some in ill-health, some are members of the majority ethnicity and religion, others not. In other words, even under this unrealistically pessimistic set of assumptions, we would already have significantly widened the circle of people participating to include a much broader set of interests than were previously represented and which are closer to the interests of other members of society not yet participating than (pivotally) *they were before*. Even a fairly affluent pensioner does not have all that much to gain from tax havens or complete healthcare privatization, for example. Even just dealing with two issues such as these would open up a flood of increased resources for others, and this is why even an initial change of this magnitude is certainly worthwhile. It represents a significant chink in the dam that will only widen, and it does so while maintaining the positive aspects of self-selection and participation as a voluntary, somewhat effortful task.

The other objection to pay-for-participation is entirely the opposite – that no one should be paid to participate as this pollutes the sanctity of the democratic process and/or that it is too expensive.

Oligarchs, in fact, have opposed pay for participation since the Parthenon was being built, equating it with 'greed and laziness'.[13] However, while participation should be an effort, it should not be an insurmountable effort and it should also be acknowledged that the kind of consideration and effort required by democracy is itself a form of work, work that citizens should be compensated for.

After all, under the current rules of representative democracy elected politicians also get paid for their labour. In some countries, like Great Britain, there was a time when they weren't. And during that time elected MPs from less-affluent backgrounds could face great difficulty in taking up their seats, because they couldn't, as the saying is, quit their day job.

Under a digital democracy, no one would need to quit their day job. But it might be convenient to hire a babysitter for a few hours or to order pizza instead of cooking supper or refrain from taking an opportunity to work overtime or take the toll route home from work. This is where pay-for-participation comes in. It's meant to help you over those little difficulties and save you the time and effort you need in order to participate. No pay at all means that, at least as things stand, time-poor members of society will participate less than they would naturally desire to and that means that changes in line with majority interests are likely to be implemented at a somewhat slower and more skewed rate than would otherwise be the case. Perhaps more importantly, it means that we would eventually run into more difficulty in maintaining high participation numbers without an immediate counteracting incentive in place (money) to combat exhaustion, laziness and general procrastination. We are, after all, only human and we have to take that into account in our plans. It may be nice to think of democracy as a noble endeavour unaffected by the vulgarity of money, but it isn't realistic. Pay and stamina go hand in hand.

There are two basic options for instituting pay-for-participation.

The first – the cheap option – is simply to crack down

on tax havens and use the increased revenues to support participation. This is why, as in Athens, we are unlikely to see pay-for-participation occur before any sort of mass participation. It is the beginnings of mass participation that create the laws that open up the gates for more. Therefore, it is more likely that we would start with a somewhat widened spectrum of participation, which frees up more resources for general use, which allows more participation, which frees up more resources (in other words, it would be the reverse of the wealth leading to power cycle that exists in electoral politics).

Tax evasion presents itself as a good source of revenue for this endeavour, because tax evasion is already a crime and it is relatively easy to uncover by bribing workers in the banking industry. Most Western countries lose billions to tax evasion every year. For example, Canada loses around $8 billion a year, enough to pay Canadians $60 per decision-making session at a 15 per cent participation rate, while Britain loses £5 billion a year, enough to pay out £27 a session to participants. If one wanted to increase this, and I would suggest we should, the answer would lie in closing the tax gap. Modern states fail to collect a lot more tax than just outrightly evaded taxes. The UK misses out on £35 billion of tax revenue a year, enough to pay £185 or three times the daily minimum wage to each participant at a 15 per cent participation rate, while Germany loses $13 billion annually, enough to pay 15 per cent of voters €52 per session.[14] This is an utterly painless method of funding what would already be extensive participation, and if participation numbers were initially to be higher than expected, one could simply pay each participant somewhat less. That will either result in reaching a stable supply-and-demand point between pay and participation or in motivating voters to find better financing options. And that is our next step anyway, as the better long-term – more expensive – option is to link pay-for-participation to receiving universal basic income or tax breaks, meaning that each time a person participated in an online decision, they would be entitled to receive a tax credit or tranche of universal basic income. Indeed, such suggestions have been made by supporters of universal basic income for years.[15] With blockchain, hashing and electronic ID verification (already in use in Estonia), such a system would be secure and it would save much of the bureaucracy, means-testing and injustices present in the welfare systems current in many states. Universal basic income could be funded in multiple ways: increased taxes on the means of production (particularly in an age of automation); dividends from national resources (something that may require re-nationalization in some instances); dramatically increased inheritance tax; or a combination of the above.

These are obviously significant economic changes, and this is why rather than democracy being something one can implement instantaneously, it is something where one step – increased participation – leads to another step – some pay for participation, crack down on tax evasion – to another step – more broad-based participation – to another step – reform of the 'welfare' system, more even distribution of wealth – to another step – better pay for participation, etc. The only important factor is that each step leads to weakening oligarchy and strengthening democracy. But since these are *major* changes, it would not be unusual for years to pass in achieving each of them. Yet each of them makes the next step easier and each step incentivizes the next step. This is why it is a *system*, not just a set of recommendations.

So, to recap so far: a real democracy, one where people actually directly affect decisions in a real and measurable way, would necessitate mass participation in those decisions – something that fortunately can be accomplished by using online platforms that already exist and by ensuring that people receive a modest material incentive that enables them to take the time they need to fully participate.

3 *Focused, outcome-oriented deliberation*
(information, isegoria *and conflict resolution)*

Mass democracy does not just require mass voting and pay to enable participation. It also requires mass deliberation, debate, discussion or, at the very least, *some reasonably complete method of putting everything on the table and hashing out differences.* Unfortunately, few things have such a poor reputation these days as online debate. Indeed, many would argue that little speaks against the idea of mass democracy as strongly as the toxic internecine warfare of social media platforms. Twitter, Facebook and myriad news sites have all too often become the new arenas for the kind of petty, mud-slinging, back-biting wars of attrition that drove so many people out of small-town committees and party politics to begin with. Constructive, useful deliberation that attracts people instead of turning them away is – most people would agree – a very different thing from this.

However, up to this point, we have not had an adequate guide for enabling such deliberation in our societies, because the need to channel large flows of information and negotiate huge swathes of public opinion in a non-hierarchical manner has never previously arisen in modern history. The institutions that facilitate public debate today were, for obvious reasons, designed to deal with a completely different set of circumstances. But this is exactly where a grasp of history really shows its value, because we do know of a society that had to grapple with the very difficulties we are facing today: Athens.

In Athens, the need to mediate public opinion on a daily basis gave rise to *two* forms of freedom of speech: *parrhesia*, which meant the freedom to express your own opinion, and *isegoria*, which meant your right to address citizens gathered in public bodies for the purposes of decision-making. *Isegoria*, for example, covered each Athenian's right to give their opinion on a law being debated in Assembly.

Up until very recently, we have only enjoyed *parrhesia* in modern societies – we are free to complain about the government to our friends and family members, for example. But we have not had, and still do not have, a *right* to public speech in the style of the Athenians. The average person cannot, for example, shuffle down to Parliament and give a speech during Question Time if they feel like it.

And rightly so.

Efficiency has traditionally demanded that public political speech be a limited commodity. But one of the key side-effects of this is that, intentionally or unintentionally, it gave the impression of a much higher level of public support for official statements and views than probably ever existed, and led to a markedly lower incidence of noticeably contested events. Traditionally, when an event occurred (a flood, for example, or a food safety scandal), it was reported on by one or two newspapers, commented on by one or two officials and that was it. Life may not always have been simple, but at least it gave that appearance in the established record. Limited conversation was all that was possible, both in politics and in media. There simply wasn't *room* for anything else.

Thus, without having to explicitly say so, our electoral-representative 'democracy' functioned on the assumption that public communication was almost completely top-down. There was no *isegoria*. And, as a result, everything seemed comparatively peaceful.

It is therefore easy to see why some people want to return to a previous pre-Internet 'golden age' when (in their view) 'our media systems deliberately promoted truth, by encouraging ethical journalism that had very strong incentives to publish the truth'.[16]

Everything was more straightforward back then, wasn't it?

But was it truthful?

That is a very different question.

Quite aside from all the trashy magazines that used to let us know which trailer park Elvis was living in and where one might find the most recent spate of two-headed calves or bug-eyed aliens, I can think of one or two other events in the world of journalism that may have indicated a slightly weaker commitment to 'truth' than those who want to hark back to the glory days might care to remember.

There's the 1989 coverage of the Hillsborough disaster, for example, an event in which ninety-six people were crushed and/or asphyxiated to death in a soccer stadium in Sheffield due to faulty crowd management and a poor emergency response. In order to escape blame for their negligence, police reported that the disaster was caused by hooliganism and drunkenness on the part of the victims and some sectors of the media helped them, even inventing tales about soccer fans looting victims and attacking rescue workers.[17]

Then there was Andrew Gilligan's famous 2003 BBC report that claimed the British government had intentionally exaggerated Iraq's weapons capabilities. The report alleged that the government knew there were doubts about the veracity of their information on Iraq's weapons programme but insisted on having it included in its war dossier in order to influence public opinion in favour of the US-led invasion of Iraq. The intelligence community, so it was alleged, had not wanted the information included as it rested on a single source that they did not consider credible.[18] After Gilligan's report came out, not only was he forced to resign, but BBC Director General Greg Dyke and Chairman Gavyn Davies were, too. In fact, the BBC apologized on the national airwaves for having engaged in bad journalism, because ... they had relied on a single source.

Although the report on the exaggerated Iraq War dossier has since been proven in essence to be correct by the rather cost-intensive method of invading Iraq and searching for weapons of mass destruction for fifteen years without finding any, back in the good old days, the BBC – the kind of media that had 'strong incentives to publish the truth' – knuckled to government pressure with scarcely a ripple on what was an extremely important public interest question – nothing, in fact, less than war.

And there's not just the Second Iraq War, there's also the first one (sometimes referred to as the Gulf War) and the infamous Nayirah testimony. In October 1990, Nayirah, a teenage Kuwaiti girl, testified before the US Congress that Iraqi soldiers, who had invaded Kuwait earlier that year, were throwing babies out of incubators in Kuwaiti hospitals and leaving them to die. The claim was reported widely and used to mobilize American opinion for the subsequent Gulf War. What *wasn't* reported was that Nayirah was a member of the Kuwaiti royal family and daughter of the Kuwaiti Ambassador to the United States, and that her testimony was arranged as part of a $10 million PR campaign conducted by professional firm Hill and Knowlton for their client the Kuwaiti government. Whether her parents really allowed 15-year-old Nayirah to remain in Kuwait to work under an assumed name as a volunteer in a hospital during a full-scale invasion, as Hill and Knowlton later claimed when her identity was finally revealed to the public after the war, is up for debate. What is pretty certain, however, is that the incubator story was a fabrication.[19] Apparently, it simply did not occur to hundreds of truth-seeking journalists to ask how a 15-year old Kuwaiti girl had managed to surface in the USA and gain access to Congress.

While conventional journalism has had its great truth-revealing moments – the *New York Times* decision to publish the Pentagon Papers in 1971 springs to mind – there's definitely a chequered record when reporting 'the truth', primarily because journalists, like everyone else, often have conflicting incentives and their own blind spots to grapple with.

And those biases have not been without effect.

Conventional media has, since its inception, systematically tarred the image of 'welfare queens', 'black gangs' (and other ethnic minorities who are disproportionately referred to as criminals), communists, Jews, Russians and anyone else who is *persona non grata*. Women have not been inherently silly and helpless for the past several hundred years, any more than black people have inherently been criminals, yet mass media – which 'deliberately promote[s] truth, by encouraging ethical journalism'[20] – has consistently and casually portrayed them this way, indeed editing them into that cookie-cutter shape, if necessary.

Thus, one of the prime complaints about social media, that it leads to conflating accounts and confusion about what the ultimate 'truth' is, isn't necessarily a bad thing. Life is complicated, and we don't have, and never have had, miraculously infallible media institutions with spotless track records. A world without *isegoria* wasn't, it turns out, all that great. It's all been rather more hit-and-miss, sometimes with horrific consequences.

As a result, there really isn't any issue that could not benefit from greater nuance and deeper understanding and it is precisely the Internet's unlimited space and low costs that permit the kind of wider-ranging deliberation that is necessary for real democracy.

A good example is a series of tweets posted by historian Abdullah Al-Arian (@anhistorian) on Twitter in November 2017 that were threaded by Esha (@esha Legal) a day later. Al-Arian, an assistant professor based in Qatar, had been irked by a *New York Times* article describing Saudi Crown Prince Mohammed bin Salman as a 'reformist' and took it upon himself to 'correct the record' by tweeting something in the range of 100 photos of *New York Times* articles uncritically covering various Saudi leaders in virtually identical language over the course of the past seventy years. These ranged from the 1953 'Arabia Preparing for Extensive Reform', which claimed that '51-year-old King Saud Ibn Abdul Aziz' is '[m]ore progressive and international-minded than his autocratic father', over 1963, when Crown Prince Faisal wrested power unto himself and was said to be on the verge of implementing local councils that 'may turn out to be the first step toward creating forms of representation', while the powers of the religious police 'appear to be on the wane'.[21] Articles from 1975 claimed that the now deceased Faisal 'led Saudis into the 20th century',[22] and promised that the new King, Khalid, would broaden participation and modernize government.[23] Perhaps unsurprisingly, in 1982, Khalid's successor, King Fahd, was also described as 'progressive and modernizing',[24] a trend that continued through the early 1990s. Dozens of articles later, Al-Arian and Esha were still going, tweeting copies of 'A Promise of Reform in Saudi Arabia' from February 2009, which stated that 'King Abdullah may finally be ready to fulfil his promise to lead his country toward greater tolerance and modernity'; 'The Other Arab Awakening'[25] from 2013, which claimed that while some Arab states might be getting revolutions, the Gulf States, including Saudi Arabia, were getting an 'evolution'; and 'A Promising New Path for Saudi Arabia', penned by the editorial board in April 2016 and which promised that Mohammed bin Salman would revolutionize the country's economy 'in ways that offer tantalizing hints at even broader reforms'.

Esha signed off with the comment: '2057: Can flying cars curb religious police's powers? 2117: Saudis to reform religious police in their Mars colony.'

Competing interpretations on current events, such as the *New York Times* versus Prof. Al-Arian's dispute on the likelihood of Saudi reforms, may make policy choices more uncomfortable, but were we really better off when there was only one script? Would deliberation really be enhanced if Al-Arian could only have made his case if invited to do so by a television station or newspaper rather than simply getting on his Twitter account?

However, rather than accept a widened debate, in which people like Al-Arian can get their oar in, whether they have been invited to or not, it has been characteristic of 'elites' to exaggerate the ill-effects of online debate by self-victimizing and denouncing anyone who disagrees with them as a 'troll' – a person whose arguments are spurious and ill-intentioned and who therefore deserves to be marginalized. By these tactics, elites seek to re-exclude people from debate by pronouncing their contributions worthless.

A good example of this is a Tweet written by Harvard lecturer Yascha Mounk shortly after a former Russian-British double agent and his daughter (Sergei and Julia Skripal) were found to have ingested a nerve agent with serious but nonfatal consequences in the city of Salisbury in England. Several days after the incident, the British government advised anyone who had visited a shopping area around the same time as the Skripals on the day they were poisoned to wash their clothing. Mounk translated this as:

Yascha Mounk ✔
@Yascha_Mounk

Russia just poisoned 500 people in the middle of the UK.

Jeremy Corbyn's response?
- Not a word of criticism.
- Blame Tories.
- UK "shouldn't let tensions get worse"
- We need "dialogue" with Russia.

Reminder for my lefty friends: Corbyn equals Jill Stein, not Bernie Sanders.

3:35 PM - 12 Mar 2018

By 6pm (GMT) on 15 March 2018, the tweet had garnered 574 replies, most of them from British people upset by Mounk's claim that 500 people had been poisoned, as well as his portrayal of Corbyn's reaction.

As of that time, the following was the first, seemingly perfectly sane, exchange of comments under Mounk's tweet:

> I'd love to see a source for 500 being poisoned. So far it's roughly 1 per cent of that number … Fwiw, I'd love @jeremycorbyn to be as passionate and open as @ SenSanders but in lieu of that, he's still light years ahead of any so called "moderate"(ly disguised Tory)
> *ToffTwits@ToffTwits – Mar 12*

> That would be the 500 pub goers warned to wash their clothes and belongings. I suppose put at risk would be

180

better, but when taking about a deadly nerve agent that's splitting hairs.
Simon P Castle@SimonPCastle – Mar 12

I sincerely hope that a tiny minority of those who frequented those establishments have any residue on clothing etc. As the CMO's statement made clear, such a risk is theoretical and the fact that hospital's have not been inundated speaks loudly that <<500 were poisoned.
ToffTwits@ToffTwits – Mar 12

I do agree, there is a bit of hyperbole going on, but doesn't change the fact that it seems highly probable that Russia deployed a chemical weapon on British soil, putting British citizens at risk. Needs a strong response and not really time for party politics.
Simon P Castle@SimonPCastle – Mar 12

Agree. So it's the all the more disappointing to see the opening tweet and the subsequent attention it doesn't merit.
ToffTwits@ToffTwits – Mar 12]/ex[

So to recap:
'Elite' Harvard lecturer: '500 people were poisoned!'
Ordinary person: 'There's a bit of hyperbole going on.'
Scrolling down, some of the meanest tweets to be found were:

The term 'Fake News' is massively over-used, but you @ Yascha_Mounk are 'Fake News'.
Tom (AAV)@Angry_Voice – Mar 13

This is an outrageous slur that you should be ashamed of. Firstly, it's not even close to 500 people and secondly, Russia is a nuclear power. If the UK or anyone else is going to accuse Russia of chemical warfare, then the evidence should be irrefutable rather than it's 'likely'.

Digital Copyright @DigCopyright – Mar 12

Oh no Putin poisoned everyone in the UK!!!!!!!!! But somehow Jeremy Corbyn survived so now I guess he's the loneliest prime minister ever

NateVerified account@inthesedeserts – Mar 13

A very small number of people called Mounk a liar, but since he did, in fact, tell a lie (500 people were definitely not poisoned, either by Russians or anyone else), this seems fair in the circumstances. In addition, many of the replies disputed Mounk's account of Corbyn's allegedly uncritical response with several people posting the official written record of Corbyn's speech in Parliament which Mounk had oversimplified.

And what happened next?

Did Mounk say 'All right, all right. Maybe I was a bit hyperbolic and perhaps it was slightly irresponsible of me to reduce a high-profile speech by a major politician that was delivered in an extremely delicate crisis situation down to a few words'?

No.

He did not do that.

He dismissed all of these people, some of whom were tweeting from Salisbury itself, as trolls.

Yascha Mounk ✔
@Yascha_Mounk

The trolls really have come out in response to this post. My favorite one so far: "Salisbury is not in the middle of the UK!"*

---

* This was one of my favourites, too, and had caused me to Google the location of Salisbury – it's close to England's south coast – nowhere near the middle.

Mounk then doubled down on his position, retweeting from Atlantic editor David Frum:

Yascha Mounk ✔
@Yascha_Mounk

An important point: Russia can meddle in our elections, or poison people on our streets, because we let it. And we let Russia do this because we are so deeply divided, with some politicians--Trump in the US, Corbyn in UK, Schröder in Germany--willing to do Russia's bidding.

> **David Frum** ✔ @davidfrum
> Big as Russia looks on the map, worth keeping in mind: its GDP = Belgium + the Netherlands. Its rulers' wealth is stashed overseas, usually in places where Western Govts cd freeze it. Its interference in Western elections launched on platforms subject to Western govt regulation

At no point does it seem to have even crossed Mounk's mind that his own behaviour could go rather beyond 'trolling' and amount to actually defaming Jeremy Corbyn, considering that he twisted Corbyn's reaction to the Skripal affair before retweeting an evidence-free claim that the leader of Britain's official opposition party is committing treason by working for a foreign government.

Contrary to much elite opinion, Internet debate has not been all bad – it is a *good* thing that we no longer live in a world where people simply have no choice but to silently accept when someone tells them (for no apparent reason and without a shred of evidence) that 500 people have been poisoned by foreign agents in the middle of the UK and that the leader of a major party is taking orders from Russia. It is a *good* thing that debate is wider and more inclusive than it once was. It's a good thing that ordinary citizens can confront elites about their statements and demand evidence for their positions. This is, in fact, what debate and deliberation are all about and we should welcome these changes, rather than being horrified by them.

However, that being said, all is still far from perfect.

Social media has created *something* like *isegoria* – the days of passive acceptance of elite opinion are definitely over – but there is still a major problem: the changes in public deliberation have not been accompanied by any kind of constructive focus or accountability.

Athenians did not practise *isegoria* – in other words, they didn't hang around debating things – just for the lulz. They practised *isegoria* as a means of getting to a decision that they intended to execute.

Despite the vast time distance between Athens and today, this is more in line with how people behave in real life than current digital deliberation is. In real life, very few people insist on continuing an argument past its sell-by date with people it is obvious they disagree with. Instead, eventually, a group will generally reach a resolution point and take a decision whether or not everyone is happy with the outcome.

But social media has no resolution mechanism – it's just one eternal argument that ends in trolling and back-biting as often as it does in edifying dialogue or informative commentary. The real problem with social media is not 'fake news' – indeed, there's no tangible quality difference between conventional and social media in this regard – it's the fact that eternal squabbling to no real purpose discourages many people from participating and offers no incentive for those who do choose to participate to do so constructively.

This is why in a real, participatory democracy, people could and likely would continue to debate on social media sites as a form of *parrhesia* – speech between citizens that does not occur in a public decision-making capacity. But this would need to be complemented by a modern version of *isegoria* that serves to facilitate deliberation in a formal environment with the explicit goal of reaching a conclusion to that debate. This could be accomplished by giving people a few hours to deliberate measures in a formal online environment before voting on binding measures. Limiting the timeframe for formal discussion and raising the stakes by ensuring that deliberation concludes with a meaningful decision-point should encourage self-filtering, but procedural rules could also be implemented: time limits on speaking; a requirement that someone who wants to speak about a technical topic has formal qualifications in that area; having people vote in advance for who should get to speak or determining who should speak by random selection from people who have put themselves forward; and mandating compulsory attendance during discussion in order to be permitted to vote.

Indeed, various methods could be used to encourage the maximum amount of deliberation among participants. People could, for example, debate in smaller, randomly assigned groups. These could be of any size (ten people, a hundred people), and could be composed completely randomly or on the basis of representing certain segments of society (e.g., age, gender, ethnicity). It would be possible to confine deliberation and voting to these smaller groups (and simply tabulate voting in the end) or allow for a mix of, say, ninety minutes of deliberation in small groups followed by ninety minutes of deliberation on the 'national' level.* Alternatively, one could have deliberation in small groups, but use a split screen that allows each individual to simultaneously monitor conversation in other groups. Or one could randomly re-mix small deliberation groups at fixed intervals. In other words, there are a lot of possibilities for encouraging a deliberative process that gives as many people as possible a chance to contribute, while also hearing from a wide variety of others, and that can be trialled and optimized according to the situation. The only truly important point is that, whatever exact form it takes, conversation is not held for its own sake but in order to come to a decision.

Democracy, contrary to received wisdom, is not actually about asking people for their opinion. In a political sense, opinions are virtually meaningless hypothetical constructs, untethered to any consequences. Democracy is about asking people what they intend to *really* do in the real world. When people need to come up with concrete solutions, they also need to focus on specifics. That shifts the debate from taking a position (which can often be learned by rote) to the difficulty of coming up with a workable policy, something that indirectly enables and incentivizes each citizen to gather and maintain a much higher level of knowledge than is presently the case. Reaching decisions that are then implemented also forces participants to eliminate some chains of action, to narrow down their focus, and to check back and assess

---

* Remember, as discussed in Part II, over a lifetime, this really adds up to an enormous level of participation.

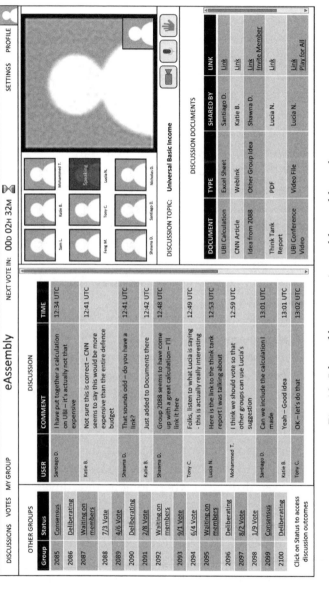

Fig. 13 Idea of how an eAssembly could work

if their judgements were correct, something that in turn creates its own data that constrains future narratives and decision-making into a more manageable spectrum.

The technology to facilitate more structured, accountable mass deliberation already exists. Postwaves and Appgree, for example, allow random distribution of participants into small discussion groups. Kialo, which uses a visual, written format, arranges comments on a statement that is being deliberated into 'pros' and 'cons', with the comments placed in descending order according to the upvotes they receive from other users. Comments *about* those comments are then nested, meaning that each user first gets a quick overview of the main arguments and issues and can then choose to deep-dive into more detail. An organizational flowchart at the top of the page lets each user know where they are in the discussion at any given time.

For example, on a discussion about universal basic income (UBI), one can see several claims, including: 'A UBI is more efficient and effective than traditional welfare programmes' and the obviously contradictory 'UBIs that meet the poverty line are too expensive for governments to afford'. Clicking on either of these claims allows the user to dive more deeply into what other participants have to say about the affordability and cost-effectiveness of universal basic income, and one can keep drilling down as long as the conversation continues.

Ideally, deliberation would occur face-to-face (similar to a Skype format), but software like Kialo could also be used as a helpful method of orienting discussion.

Getting deliberation right does not require censorship or heavy-handed attempts to shut down contributions one does not agree with. What it does require is that conversation – which, after all, serves the function of mediating society-wide conflict – be tethered to reality rather than occurring in a consequence-free vacuum.

4 Precarious, informal leadership (but leadership all the same)

Despite its essentially egalitarian nature, democracy does still require informal leadership, and it is essential that it strikes a balance between providing that leadership and the ability to take collective action.

Some people don't like to hear this, but while democracy in Athens furnished an extraordinary level of equality when it came to voting on each issue and the right to address citizens in public decision-making bodies, not by a million miles did each Athenian possess exactly the same political clout – and it is likely that this would be the case in a modern democracy, too.

This should not overshadow the fact that there *were* plenty of opportunities for the obscure individual to have a real political impact in Athens – people who may have only addressed the Assembly or brought a case to court once in their lives, but who held sway on that issue – but there were also people who were particularly articulate and who could call on an impressive level of accomplishments and expertise to back up their arguments. These people, sometimes referred to as *rhetors*, were essentially full-time democrats, constantly speaking for and against motions, bringing court cases and exercising their opportunities to hold office to the full. Due to the voluntary nature of much of Athenian participation, one could, without exaggeration, say that some of these individuals dominated the political scene, and they often came from, or had at least acquired, some wealth. The playing field of Athenian democracy, in other words, was a lot less tilted than it is today, but it definitely wasn't entirely flat.

The *key* to the maintenance of a meaningful degree of political equality in Athens, and the main differentiator to electoral politics today, was that *rhetors* held no official position. Their power was purely a factor of how much other people respected their opinions. And *because* their clout was purely informal, no matter how famous and influential a *rhetor* might be, they still had to win consent for every single thing that they wanted to do, no matter how trivial. And winning that consent was no easy task. Anyone could get up and disagree with even the most illustrious *rhetor* (and people often did) and famous *rhetors* could lose motions to absolute nobodies (and they did).

Being a prominent *rhetor* was thus not necessarily an easy calling, and, to make matters worse, there were no direct material advantages tied to it. Unlike politicians today, and unlike the executive officials of Athens, *rhetors* did not draw a salary. What you got out of being a *rhetor* was mainly fame and glory, and even getting that much was a risky business. An ordinary citizen could show up to Assembly or the courts and vote and they would get paid and go home none the worse for wear. The same was not always true of someone who argued on a motion or who brought a lawsuit. Such persons could be punished for giving 'bad advice' in Assembly or stripped of their participatory rights if their lawsuit was found to be spurious.

As one can see, life as a *rhetor* really was quite

uncertain, and it is precisely this informal, precarious leadership that could benefit democracy today.

We know, for example, that it had a very salutary effect on Athenian policy. While persons of great wealth or education were often overrepresented in official debates, the decisions themselves were in the hands of the masses. And it is certainly no coincidence (nor was it seen to be one at the time) that in Athens, substantial taxation was something that only afflicted the affluent. And not only did they pay up on their taxes, wealthy Athenians also often engaged in unofficial philanthropy beyond what was owed. This was not necessarily because they were good people, it was just common sense: those kinds of bonus points came in handy when you found yourself in front of an Assembly or jury composed of hoi polloi. The very circumstance in which decisions were made by large numbers of ever-changing people in Assembly or the courts (rather than by a small number of elected or lottery-selected officials) meant that the only sensible strategy for gaining advantage was to ingratiate oneself with people generally through some sort of societal contribution. In other words, rather than pure high-mindedness and noble restraint, it was something as prosaic and unglamorous as the numbers involved in decision-making coupled with the precarious nature of leadership that channelled greed and self-interest into generosity and civic duty.

This demonstrates the advantages of informal, precarious democratic leadership over formal, relatively stable leadership (for example, that acquired via election). But while it may be a good thing to keep leaders on the ropes, it is still good to *have* leaders (as opposed to an utterly egalitarian, leaderless society), because, however much work everyone else is doing, leaders tend to do even more of it and take even more personal risks – and someone has to do that kind of thing.

Whatever else you want to say about the kind of people who want to become political leaders, or, as the Athenians would have said, *rhetors*, they are often great catalysts for getting things done.

In fact, one of the most famous stories about Athens illustrates the advantages of a people's democracy led by inspiring, driven, ambitious, glory-hungry, sometimes slightly crazy, *rhetors*.

In 483 BC, just as democracy was really beginning to get under way, the Athenians experienced a stroke of good luck; the state-owned silver mines had hit a bonanza and the city was awash with cash. Some people suggested that this abundance should be distributed among the citizens,[26] a measure that would have translated into a payment equivalent to several thousand dollars per family. This suggestion was countered by another proposal, put in by a man named Themistocles. Themistocles proposed that no Athenian citizen would receive a single cent from the mines, but that the windfall should be spent on building a state-of-the-art fleet of warships instead. These ships would not only be advantageous for the usual, perpetually ongoing local conflicts, but would definitely also come in handy if Athens were ever attacked by greater powers.

Confronted with this choice between receiving a considerable bonus in the very near future or building a fleet of warships on this scale (something they had never done before) and retraining for an entirely new kind of warfare in the interests of national security, the Athenians voted for short-term self-sacrifice in the hopes of long-term gain. They backed Themistocles' plan and built the ships.

Three years later King Xerxes of Persia launched an invasion of Greece. Considering that Persia was an extremely large and powerful nation, this was pretty much the worst possible scenario for the Athenians. Together with the other Greek states that had decided to fight Xerxes, they manned their new navy to the full and attempted to defeat the Persians at sea, a gamble that required them to leave the city of Athens undefended. In other words, rather than plod along as navel-gazing peasants, the Athenians decided to embark on a daring, high-risk strategy that put everything behind defeating Xerxes with their new navy.

And they did.

At the Battle of Salamis – possibly one of the most crucial battles of history – the Athenian navy clobbered the Persians.

By staking it all on Themistocles' highly ambitious and expensive strategy, which had required the citizens to freely agree to short-term self-sacrifice, the Athenians secured not just their own survival, but Greek pre-eminence in south-eastern Europe, giving breathing space to a civilization that has influenced Western culture to this day, and confirming their faith in *demokratia* – people power.

However – inspiring as it is – the story isn't just about 'the people' who forsook a generous dividend payment in order to build the new war fleet. It is also about Themistocles himself, Themistocles the *rhetor*.

Themistocles was by no means a humble every-man, but a highly, perhaps even ruthlessly, ambitious person,[27] determined to risk all to defeat Persia and to get everyone else to put themselves at risk, too. What is more, Themistocles' evidence, case studies and footnotes for his plan of war were somewhat lacking. In fact, his talent lay in 'intuitively meeting an emergency' and 'passing adequate judgement in matters in which he had no experience'.[28] Themistocles, in other words, was a gut-feeling kind of guy, and, convinced of his own assessment, he did not hesitate to turn on the charm and even twist things a little in order to get his motion to build those ships through.[29]

'Now, whether by accomplishing this he did injury to the integrity and purity of public life or not', Plutarch later wrote, 'let the philosopher rather investigate. But that the salvation which Hellenes achieved at that time came from the sea, and that it was those very triremes* which restored again the fallen city of Athens, Xerxes himself bore witness.'[30]

Themistocles supplied the vision, and the citizens – who had to buy into his plan – supplied the force to achieve it. It is unlikely that we would be hearing so much about Athens today if it weren't for these two equally important but distinct contributions. And, funnily enough, a lot of the times we remember as our 'best' democratic moments bear a striking resemblance to the story of Themistocles and the Ships.

Anti-democrats, such as sortitionists, who worry about overrepresentation from highly educated and articulate speakers,[31] are barking up the wrong tree. Not only are two of their most despised figureheads, Donald Trump and Nigel Farage, notable for their lack of charisma, getting fired up isn't always a bad thing. Martin

---

* Those would be the ships.

Luther King Jr.'s 'I have a dream', Winston Churchill's 'We shall fight on the beaches' and JFK's 'We're going to land a man on the moon because it's hard' speeches were all about vision, visions that didn't have a whole lot behind them other than conviction and strength of character, but were somehow still more powerful than all the flowcharts, plans and analyses in the world. They did not give society details: they gave society a direction and a goal. And if it takes a confident, highly articulate, educated person to do this kind of thing, so be it.

Democracy in any form is always going to need people like this and this is why we need to leave room for unofficial leaders. While it distributes voting power on each issue to every person equally, democracy still leaves the deliberation space open for some people to become highly influential for a day or a year or a decade. The trick of democracy is to ensure that such people have the ability to play an informal role in democracy (for example, in opinion-forming), but deny them any formal authority.

This means that participatory democracy, in the long run, cannot coexist with any mechanism via which some people are authorized to speak for others or to cast votes for others. Such a practice gives ambitious would-be *rhetors* far too much power and would touch off the same kind of wealth translating into power translating into wealth cycle that currently exists in electoral politics. But it also means that a purely sortitionist state with no leadership continuity is also unlikely to function. *Rhetors* do contribute and they need the space to do it in.

Implementing the first three steps outlined in this part of the book (enable mass, online decision-making;

pay-for-participation; formalize deliberation into the decision-making process) provides for this by ensuring that participation is voluntary and that deliberation, both at a formal and informal level is free and open. That this will enable the most articulate and able a certain prestigious position – provided they are willing to work for it – is an intended consequence.

5 Sortition in its proper place

Although plans to replace legislative functions with small-scale sortition are misguided, sortition still has an important role to play in democracy. In fact, the changes that we are experiencing through technology make some forms of sortition well suited to meeting our current governance needs.

There are several ways that sortition could be constructively incorporated into a mass participatory democracy.

It could, for example, be used to perform executive tasks. The difference between legislative and executive posts in our current system can sometimes be easy to confuse. The general rule is that representatives debate and pass laws which are then executed, or enforced, by officials – the police force, for example, or the health and safety board or the revenue service. However, in some electoral systems, the government – that is, the Prime Minister and the cabinet – are also elected legislators. These people therefore exercise a dual function: they represent their constituents and vote on laws in Parliament, but they also head a certain section of the state administration, for example, the Department of Justice or of Education. As the ultimate overseer of their department, each minister is ultimately responsible for its work (which is why ministers are sometimes required to resign after a scandal). In other countries, the USA for example, the difference between executive and legislative is more clear-cut: the President appoints the most senior officials, e.g. Secretary of State, Secretary of Defense, etc.

Whatever form this takes, it is these executive positions and their functions that are prime candidates for sortition in participatory democracy. And that is not nearly as weird as it at first sounds.

As things stand now, the vast majority of elected representatives are not subject matter experts in any particular area: there are plenty of justice ministers without a law degree; health ministers without medical expertise; and finance ministers without any deep grasp of accounting or economics. However, they still manage to do the job they are appointed to do: exercise oversight over their department and ensure that it acts in conformity with the wishes of government. How that *exactly* happens is often left to the civil servants who work under them in the department or in related agencies and regulatory bodies and who often exercise some discretion in interpreting each case they are confronted with in conformity with the laws.

This is how countries manage to keep running for months or even years at a time when parties fail to form a government after an election. The work of governing, e.g., revenue collection, registering births and deaths, the military and consular services, pollution monitoring, the post office, central banks (the 'Fed' in the US) just keep ticking over.

Up until now, all I have suggested in this book is to switch out elected politicians for mass decision-making. In other words, I have suggested changing the composition of the legislature. Civil servants, regulatory bodies and every other facet of a modern state would remain in place underneath mass participatory democracy, just like before. Regulatory bodies would go on regulating; federal agencies would continue their agenting; central banks would keep distributing money and adjusting interest rates.

What is *missing*, however, is the connecting link between this vast bureaucracy and mass decision-making: the top layer of the executive that oversees the translation of policy from abstract law to concrete implementation.

The question is, in a real democracy, could we and *should we* select such officials randomly, as the Athenians, for the most part, did?

There are good reasons to think that we should. Rotating office rapidly and preventing persons from being able to predict which office they may hold – something sortition is eminently suited for – helps to prevent corruption. Moreover, top executive officials, such as government ministers, primarily execute oversight and directory functions, rather than expertise functions, and these are potentially better carried out by outsiders without previous ties or agendas.

Finally, when the Athenians chose officials to execute the public will, they selected them in panels of ten, often with each official having particular responsibility for a subsection of the overall brief. In a world of increasing complexity, ten ministers of health rather than one, for example, might be more appropriate to modern needs. After all, specializations could be divided between them: one could be responsible for hospitals, one for research, a third for public health initiatives, etc. This would potentially provide more clarity to the public on various responsibilities and allow oversight to focus on multiple targets at once while still allowing for collegial coordination.

That lottery-selected officials wouldn't necessarily have any more expertise than current ministers do would not be harmful, because they would not enjoy the power to make final decisions. They would not, for example, be able to shut down a hospital or privatize health clinics unless ordered to do so by the general public, and they would not replace experts employed by the state or related agencies. They would be responsible purely for ensuring that public decisions are executed by the civil apparatus over which they exercise oversight. Sortition and mass participation used this way are not about de-professionalization; they are about striking a happy medium between professionalization and transparency that is necessary to maintaining both of these values.

Now, at this point some might object that persons selected by sortition might be incompetent.

And I freely admit, there are incompetent people around. Far be it from me to deny that.

But there are also a lot of *corrupt* people around. People who do exactly what Bryan Caplan suggested and say one thing, while acting out another. People who for example might talk all day long about how important public health is, while actually defunding the health system. People who might continuously and passionately orate on the importance of peace, while disposing over the world's greatest killing machines and stockpiling enough weaponry to kill everyone on earth multiple times over. Such people exist, and whether or not they are competent doesn't help us very much if they don't undertake the actions we wish them to undertake.

You don't need to be terribly competent to, for example, not arm jihadists. This requires virtually no competence whatsoever. You don't need to be very competent to hire revenue staff to investigate large companies, or to refrain from allowing executives to write tax regulations while on sabbatical from global accounting firms. Especially when selected in multi-person panels and supported by an enormous staff of experts (the civil servants whom we pay and who currently brief politicians), the chances of even a layperson noticing a problem with such practices are probably fairly high.

But it is also quite irrelevant, because we are not asking people selected by sortition to fill executive roles to *make* decisions, but merely to *execute* them. Let us say, for example, that a nation was to make a decision to increase resources for auditing large companies. It is not that difficult to prepare a budget for hiring and carrying out, say 25 per cent, more audits – in fact, it would not be difficult at all for the civil servants who would complete this work. Overseers are merely there to ensure that they do it, that the resources are used as efficiently as possible, and to check the quality control between efforts and results. They will, undoubtedly, from time to time need to approve minor decisions in the service of fulfilling the general aim, but this is a different sort of decision than deciding what the general aim should be.

And if I were to choose someone to *execute* a plan, I would avoid choosing too many eloquent, big ideas people, as they are rarely suited to this kind of work, and less so in combination with each other. Instead,

I'd go for quiet organizers who sit in the backroom of pubs on Wednesday evenings with a map and a compass planning the village council's submission to government for the exact train route through their area. Keeping track of things in obsessive detail is precisely what they are good at, and the only real qualification one needs for this job.

In reality, likely two kinds of people would be attracted to putting themselves forward to serve on sortition panels: the kind of person who would like to become a *rhetor*, as, of course, any position that entails accountability to the population as a whole brings with it plenty of exposure; and the kind of organizer I've referred to above. Between these factors, the involvement of multiple persons, and the ultimately merciless degree of public scrutiny that would be visited upon anyone who has to explain to the entire nation how the departmental work is going, it is unlikely that the number of dramatic mistakes would increase.

And if, for some reason, after all that being said, someone *were* to accidentally order the wrong kind of dialysis machine, then that is regrettable, but still a correctable mistake and a problem of significantly less magnitude than gradually bankrupting the entire health system while claiming that you are doing nothing of the sort – something that is currently perfectly possible.

This is the first potential use-case for sortition in modernity.

The second potential use for sortition is as a means of local government for small towns and villages. Many people who advocate change in various fields often emphasize their willingness to start with 'local' small change – precisely the wrong way to go about things. In order to be effective, mass participation would have to be implemented on a national level, because national governments set the rules that constrain all of the lower tiers of decision-making (e.g., state and municipal government).

But that begs the question: would it be necessary to have mass digital participation on every level of governance, or could small municipal governments be run by a hundred or so randomly selected volunteers who have a duty to call occasional mass decision-making meetings to ratify their programmes? Or perhaps a duty to utilize participatory budgeting? This would increase the number of people involved in local government, and assigning them tasks randomly and/or insisting on a regular turnover of participants would potentially shake up local corruption.

One hundred people out of a town population of two or ten thousand is, after all, a far greater percentage, and therefore more representative than one hundred people out of, say, sixty-five million. In a town of ten thousand people with five thousand people entitled to vote, one would get through the entire town in fifty years this way (particularly if one mandated a maximum number of years that could be served per individual), and we are, of course, requiring that an element of mass decision-making be retained on all decisions in any event – more than is currently the case.

Because this lowest level of local government has few powers and is easily constrained by higher levels of government; because it involves small numbers of people, who can thus be relatively easily represented in rotation without the same issues with corruption that surface when the ratio of decision-makers to general population is small; and because one is unlikely to be able to turn out mass participation on riveting issues like bus shelters and cemetery maintenance all that often – while I am not strongly advocating this solution, I would not rule it out, either. After all, small-town corruption is often *worse* than national corruption, if more petty. If one were to institute all the other measures that I have outlined here and come to the conclusion that there are problems on the local level – with elections or corruption, or because people don't participate as regularly on local issues – I would not rule this out as a means of alleviating the situation. It is, however, extremely important that such solutions be applied to small towns only, perhaps up to a maximum of ten thousand inhabitants. A city the size of London or New York, for example, certainly would not qualify, as their size, and more considerable powers, make them subject to all of the weaknesses of sortition that were described in Part II.

The third potential use case for sortition in a modern mass participatory democracy is to support decision-making in much the same way as the *boule* supported the Assembly in Athens: by organizing general motions for debate and keeping order during that debate. While legislating via randomly selected people is a bad idea, letting them formulate motions – provided that they are obligated to receive input from the general public during this process and that it is possible to propose amendments during debate – is a different matter. Having debate itself facilitated by randomly selected persons who keep time and order is also certainly preferable, from the point of view of preventing corruption, to having the same persons conduct this on a regular basis.

To some extent, this form of sortition (which has a proven track-record) is already in use in Ireland, where the Citizens' Assembly pre-debates on recommendations for referendum, but where, up until this point, referenda have always been held, thus ensuring the legitimacy and representativeness of the final decision.

Sortition in these three areas would not only help to prevent corruption and thus oligarchy from reforming under a digital direct democracy, it also has another effect that the Athenians definitely did not intend — it can enable demographic representativeness (e.g., age, gender and ethnic distribution) to be assured in the areas where it is used. Some aspects of democracy are a survival-of-the-fittest competition, such as holding sway as a *rhetor*, and these aspects are likely to reflect whatever power dynamic reigns in any given society. Using sortition to fill other roles in a demographically balanced way can even up the playing field in a non-authoritarian manner and counterbalance the necessity of letting the ambitious and privileged live out their aspirations on the national stage.

Sortition is a facilitator of mass participation, not a replacement of it, but it can still serve a valuable function in a democracy by counteracting corruption and engaging a higher number of citizens in executive tasks.

So, to sum up, there are five basic steps that would need to be taken to implement a direct, digital democracy that is more in keeping with modern needs than the current electoral-representative system:

1 Scale mass participation tools.
2 Pay people to participate.

3 Provide a free deliberation space prior to decision-making.
4 Harness ambition by providing informal leadership channels.
5 Use sortition to oversee executive tasks and support decision-making.

I trust this sounds at least a bit better than 'go back to vetting political candidates in smoke-filled rooms' or 'reduce laws so that people can engage in a spot of foot voting'.

However, it is important to remember that humans will always make mistakes and they'll always do things they later regret, even in a full democracy.

But that doesn't mean change is futile or without consequences. No one today would say that we live in an age with antibiotics, ergo it is a utopia. But talk to anyone old enough to remember a time without them and you'll quickly find out that while antibiotics may not have made life an *actual* utopia, compared to not having them, it certainly feels like it. Likewise, democracy may not make us angels, but in my view it is still significantly better than being gradually impoverished by an oligarchical globalized super-elite, which is where we are headed as things stand now.

And what makes this version of democracy a viable one is that it does not rely on people being better people. You can keep being greedy. You can keep being lazy. You can continue to care about your family more than perfect strangers. This is merely to be human.

When anti-democrats hold a mirror up to humanity, all they can see are all the things they perceive as flaws. And like the world's most ambitious plastic surgeon,

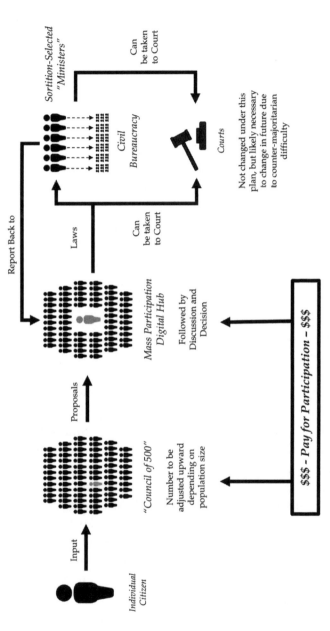

Individual Citizen

Input

"Council of 500"

Number to be adjusted upward depending on population size

Proposals

Mass Participation Digital Hub

Followed by Discussion and Decision

Report Back to

Laws

Sortition-Selected "Ministers"

Civil Bureaucracy

Can be taken to Court

Can be taken to Court

Courts

Not changed under this plan, but likely necessary to change in future due to counter-majoritarian difficulty

$$$ – Pay for Participation – $$$

Fig. 14 The Five Principles of Modern Direct Democracy

they're sure that with some snipping here and there, they'll make that reflection perfect yet.

When I hold up that mirror I see something that is perhaps imperfect, but which only exists through an interaction between itself and the outside world, between inner compulsions and external conditions that are far too complex for me to even fully comprehend much less control.

I can only try channel those forces constructively, which is why I have taken the approach that I have.

But any change, even good change, even necessary change, is still a lot of effort.

So why should we do all this? Why should we try to move from an electoral-representative democracy to a direct participatory one?

Why It's Worth It

1 People want democracy

First, most people still seem committed to the basic premise that all should be able to participate in politics and that this is more important than always having one's way. Many people seem unwilling to denigrate others merely because they disagree with them, nor do they seem ready to give up on the idea of political equality any time soon. People may want to fix democracy, but there is no great desire to do so at the expense of its basic principles.

Ben Goldacre's 'Brexit voters are racist idiots' tweet, for example, provoked many comments from his followers, such as:

You're a clever lad, don't make yourself out to be a total belm by patronising and insulting grown adults who exercised their democratic right to vote how they saw fit. It's not cool. And I voted remain.
The Doc@dr_dan_81

Always worth remembering that support for eugenics and hatred of democracy ('the mob') was widespread among scientists and intellectuals up until WW2. Academic achievement is often a stranger to empathy and decency, but not to arrogance.
InSuffolk@InSuffolk

Sadly I feel this just confirms that those felt the 'metropolitan elite' was condescending and disparaging had grounds (& I voted remain!)
PeterW@PeterW4tw – Feb 17

I voted remain, but it's unthinking snobby comments like this which helped lose us the referendum.
Michael Goodier@michaelgoodier

Similarly, comments from van Reybrouck's *Guardian* article complaining about 'poorly informed citizens' voting for Brexit and the necessity of legislating via sortition include, for example:

'There seems be a yearning amongst the North London "intelligentsia" for an al-Sisi like character: someone who'll rescue the liberals from the teeming hordes, by depriving the poor of any say in government, or worse ...'
'Drawing by lot sounds good in principle, but how do you select the experts who inform the citizens? What are their political views. How open can this process be made to be? I find it also funny that the Guardian

and other supposed "liberal" outlets have begun running articles on this subject ever since they fell on the losing side of the referendum. Democracy it seems, is only bad when you lose.'

'They conveniently neglect the question of the self interest and values of this knowledgeable technocratic elite that they obviously pine for – rule by a greedy, psychopathic, callous, but "knowledgeable" elite is apparently much to be preferred to regular democracy.'

'"Disenchanted and poorly informed citizens"? Well, I'm neither disenchanted nor poorly informed and I'm not convinced that the majority of voters were, either. When a writer starts his piece with a comment as dismissive as this, it does nothing to suggest that his views will be worth considering.'

'Well said. I will bet 1000 Euros that if the vote had gone the other way, the "remainers" would have been congratulating the well informed citizens who had examined carefully every nuance of every argument before casting their vote. These elitists sicken me. We are not all morons, in fact, in my experience, talking to normal people (something that I doubt that the London based "Guardianistas" do) I found that "leavers" had far more knowledge of the issues than "remainers". But please do not let facts interfere with you preconceived liberal prejudices. Incidentally, I voted remain.'

This general sentiment in favour of democracy is reflected in studies undertaken by the Pew Research Centre. According to its findings, while representative democracy remains the most popular form of government in most countries, majorities in nearly all nations also feel positively about direct democracy, with 66 per cent in favour worldwide. In the USA, Canada and Western Europe, support for direct democracy is even higher: 'a median of 70 per cent said it was somewhat or very good with 25 per cent saying it was very good.'[32]

Direct democracy is rarely discussed in the media, primarily because it is an unpopular idea among the traditional democratic gatekeepers – journalists, politicians and academics. When it is discussed, it is often prefaced by remarks about how 'radical', 'fringe' and 'unusual' it is. But both the numbers and general comments show that many people are not nearly as hostile to the idea of direct democracy as gatekeepers are. That shouldn't be a huge surprise: electoral democracy has served us well (it's definitely better than any form of purely 'elite' rule), so giving the system a general overhaul, especially one that can be carried out in careful steps, is certainly preferable to throwing out the baby with the bath water as the anti-democrats desire.

But there are a lot of other reasons to like real participatory democracy. In fact, even anti-democrats should find some reason to like it because ...

2 Fuller democracy solves a lot of anti-democrat objections to democracy

Interestingly, what a lot of anti-democrats say they are looking for in a system turns out to be ... democracy. It does, after all, efficiently deal with so many of the things they criticize in our current electoral-representative system.

Achen and Bartels, for example, complain that policies often take longer to bear fruit than an electoral cycle lasts and thus may be prematurely abandoned,[33] but Athenian-style democracy does not have electoral cycles, and therefore no arbitrary deadlines by when a policy needs to be a proven success. With continuously revisable decisions, it is easy to take new information into account at any point and escape the cyclical electoral process and its short-term horizons.

Other anti-democrats, like Somin, claim that in modern democracies people have no incentive to acquire knowledge in an unbiased manner or to vigorously consider it, since they are engaged in blind partisan voting.[34] But without elections, political parties would struggle to retain relevance. When everything is à la carte, there's no further need to label yourself Democrat or Republican, Labour or Conservative, or to have any loyalty to any such group. In a participatory democracy, voters don't need the approval of others in order to cast their own votes, nor are they obliged to agree with others on a long list of issues in order to have an impact. If you want to be tough on crime, but don't include drug possession in that, that's up to you. If you're against foreign wars, but want to hold on to your guns, that's OK. If you want university tuition to be free, but not healthcare, that's fine. As even the anti-democrats admit, most people aren't consistently committed to either a liberal or a conservative ideology – only the 'higher echelons of political society' are,[35] which is why they engage in obstructionist tactics when it comes to governing and work so hard to fan the flames of partisanship. Direct democracy provides a great opportunity to escape this trap.

It also provides a great opportunity to stop the obsessive and often abrupt passing and reversing of legislation that political parties are so fond of. In a direct system, after all, decisions are often more stable (since entire governments and thus government programmes do not change based on minor population fluctuations, for example, as they do now), and thus we can likely expect fewer abrupt, ideology-driven policy reversals than we currently experience. Anti-democrats may complain that people do not 'rethink their fundamental political commitments with every election cycle',[36] but quite apart from the fact that it is rather the definition of a fundamental commitment that you don't continually re-think it (marriage, for example, or having children), such commitments can be the source of great stability.

But there are other important advantages, as well.

In our present electoral system, we are asked to vote based on feeling, because we are asked to *trust* the politicians we vote for. That is an entirely different kind of decision than stating what policies you agree with. When you vote, you *don't* see a list of policies and circle the ones you want. You put a mark next to a name and, in some cases, a face. The name and the face of the person who will be running your life from now on. While, as we saw in Part I, this does not disincentivize people from informing themselves nearly as much as anti-democrats believe it does, it also fails to provide really good incentives to focus solely on the issues at hand. One needs to consider personality and authenticity as well. Thus, the logic of elections – as they actually occur – has *never been* to determine which views you line up behind. It's to determine who you trust (or distrust the least) to do things in your favour, regardless of what they are saying. This clouds the issue and makes it difficult to determine why people vote the way they do.

Is it the candidate? Or the issues? Or, more likely, some complex interaction between the two? Direct democracy eliminates this confusion and keeps things focused on the matter at hand, because it asks people which policies they support – not which politician they think will look after them.

Those are several major advantages already, but the list goes on.

Larry Bartels told a reporter that, under electoral democracy, 'we don't know how to incorporate the role of political elites in a constructive way into the governing process',[37] but Athenian-style democracy provided a contained but still important role for elites, one that encouraged them to be constructive in order to get what they wanted. This would still be the case in a future democracy, where ambitious, educated citizens would continue to play a prominent role in shaping debate as *rhetors*, but rely on citizens to make the ultimate decisions.

Finally, anti-democrats complain that people cannot be informed because they tend to talk only to those who agree with them,[38] but in a fuller, participatory democracy, this is impossible – people must debate in a country-wide forum (indeed they have huge incentives to do so), and they do so not with the goal of letting off steam or telling 'the other side off', but for a limited time under the enforced pressure of coming to a workable resolution that they will have to live with.

It turns out that, contrary to anti-democrat claims, it isn't necessary to forgo political equality in order to stop these problems. Changing the rules of the game makes much of this complained-about behaviour disappear. So if anti-democrats were really serious about all the things they *claim* to want to deal with, they'd be gung-ho for democracy.

And there are further advantages to this style of democracy that anti-democrats haven't thought of.

3 *Writing a new social contract*

Democracy, as we said before, is not a method for finding the single right answer, but rather of mediating conflict. And this is worth remembering because technology has changed more than just politics in the narrower sense. It is also bringing change in areas like privacy, labour and wealth distribution. How these issues will be dealt with in the future has not yet been resolved, and as the subject of different views and interests, they are also, obviously, the subject of conflict.

Even if we don't end up in an AI-run *I Robot* state, it is fairly obvious that facial recognition technology, web-filtering, GPS and Amazon Alexas make both shaping and suppressing political opinion much easier than was previously the case. Such technology can also, as we know, be used to target voters to a much greater extent than was possible in the past. The story of Cambridge Analytica's targeted campaign ads for Trump and Brexit's Leave campaign is well known. But even in the early days of Internet party politics, the Obama campaign was using algorithms to trawl through databases that contained up to *one thousand variables* looking for patterns on each of its 180 million voter profiles. According to one source: 'Obama's campaign began the election year [2012] confident it knew the name of every one of the 69,456,897 Americans whose votes had put him in the White House [in 2008].' The campaign used this data in a variety of ways to micro-target voters and was able to predict votes within tenths of a percentage point.[39]

The issue of privacy and surveillance spans topics like electoral law, data sovereignty, use of medical records, criminal investigations, civil disobedience hacking, safety, the right to be forgotten and much more.

We had privacy pretty much figured out back in the days when it merely involved not opening other people's mail, but we definitely don't have it figured out now, and it is uncertain if this is something that can be satisfactorily managed at all in a top-down electoral democracy.

In addition to this, we have another even stranger problem on our hands: namely, the vast increase in productivity that technology has provided. Since we no longer need to work a forty-hour week to support ourselves at the current standard of living, this has the potential to disrupt relations between labour and capital to an extent that has not been seen since the dawn of the industrial age. AI and globalization will only make answering the fundamental questions – Who has the right to money? How is that determined? And why? – all the more pressing.

All of the 'changes' that we experienced over the last few centuries were really just tinkering with the system that emerged from the last major technological wave – mechanization. We got better at doing what we were doing. We worked things into a better and fairer balance. But now we are confronted with whole new paradigms in terms of both privacy/surveillance and work/wealth distribution. We had a social contract in place for the old world – we don't have one yet for the new one.

There are thus a lot of decisions to be made in the

coming years, and it is doubtful that the electoral-representative system, which has long descended into oligarchy, is going to do a satisfactory job of making them. Just as representative democracy was necessary to mediate the changes in society after the Enlightenment, so too is a new form of politics necessary to come to grips with the challenges confronting us today.

Final Words: Buckle-up, Buttercup: The Future Is Going to be Interesting

There are a lot of reasons to be in favour of democracy – and, in fact, the future of democracy is brighter than it has ever been. Previous generations didn't have the chance we have to participate more fully in the decisions affecting us. They were trapped in a party-led system where all politics had to be channelled into rough set-menu choices for years at a time, where data was hard to come by and, at the end of the day, most things were done by best guess. What they had was certainly better than monarchy or feudalism, but it was still a thin version of democracy, with a stark differentiation between the in-crowd and the out-crowd.

Not only does future democracy not have to be that way, it is nearly inevitable that it *won't* be that way – as long as we're not taken in by anti-democrats and their gloom and doom siren song of pre-emptive defeat.

A whole new dimension of human existence – peer-to-peer communication, mass viral organization – has come into being and the current political system provides *no outlet for it*. There is nowhere for citizens to turn their common ideas into actions, nowhere for them to negotiate a new social contract and balance of societal justice in a globalized digital era. With all of the possibilities for participation that technology has enabled, the funnel of electoral-representative politics just isn't *big enough* to channel that potential. Like a water wheel sitting under Niagara Falls, it can't handle even a fraction of the load of energy directed at it.

It is unleashing chaos, yes. But also power, productivity, potential.

So rather than screaming about how unfair it is that the river suddenly got bigger, we need to get ourselves a bigger wheel.

And we're fortunate in that we have a pretty good blueprint for a very big 'democracy wheel' to hand: the democracy that existed in Athens. Some might say that is primitive, but the truth is that Athenian civilization was surprisingly sophisticated. It was, after all, a society that had got as far as mortgages, insurance plans and the kind of entertainment you tend to get from *Saturday Night Live* comedians embarking on a solo career. While their rules certainly need an update in some ways, their basic design – a democracy 'wheel' that channelled participation and decision-making across the entire society – was sound.

But achieving that kind of change requires ... well ... change. In the version of digital democracy that I have outlined in this book, gatekeepers and elites who could once rely on life-long privilege would have to adjust to fighting it out for the people's approval just like Athenian *rhetors* did. They would not be able to dismiss popular discontent with their ideas as being stupid or ignorant and simply continue to implement them anyway. In other words, digital democracy would

come with a rather abrupt levelling of the playing field
– the status of 'ordinary person' would increase and the
status of elites would decrease markedly.

It is for this reason that elites and gatekeepers are
looking so hard for excuses to prevent democracy from
developing naturally to a more participatory model.
They've tried to exclude some streams of opinion by
dividing everything and everyone into categories of
'good' and 'bad', 'superior' and 'inferior', 'respectable'
and 'trashy'; they've tried to convince us that what they
deem good is good for everyone and for all time; that
the sum total of human knowledge is already available and that there is nothing that experts do not know
or cannot measure. They've placed a double-standard
of epic proportions between themselves and ordinary
people, insisting that it is OK for 'experts' to make
major mistakes, which must be forgiven, but not for
ordinary people to do so; that their own ideas must
only be hypothetically feasible and that they defend only
their ideals, rather than how they pan out in reality.
Above all, they have tried to hollow out the idea of
democracy, claiming that it does not need people – that
somehow, in fact, people get in the way.

And after all that, they've come up empty, with nothing to show for their efforts but a few malicious claims
and envious sniping.

So don't fall for it.

Anti-democrats are just afraid of us. But although we
have history on our side, we should be afraid of them,
too.

After all, they've already mobilized a substantial
amount of resources for the last stand. Anti-democrats
are not founding institutes, pumping out editorials

attacking the idea of political equality and seeking to discredit hoi polloi because they are planning to go quietly into the night. And the only way for them to achieve their goals – continued privilege for political gatekeepers – is to roll back on the very idea of democracy, to make things worse, rather than better.

To try to get people to agree to their unholy bargain, the anti-democrats have mobilized their usual henchmen: fear, uncertainty and doubt.

Keeping with that strategy, anti-democrats will likely label the solution I have outlined in this book 'naive', 'wishful thinking' and 'unrealistic'. They will say that democracy in the sense of people power is a wonderful thought, but alas in this vale of tears 'it's just not that easy'. They'll say how many 'questions it throws up' and then they'll probably dwell on the fact that Athens had slaves, conveniently overlooking the fact that representative electoral 'democracy' was also originally a slave society. They will say these things because it *is* naive to think that, if you propagate a vision for a better future, you will be rewarded by the very people who benefit the most from ensuring that future never arrives, and for anti-democrats not being rewarded for something is the same as that thing not being possible.

But Athenian democracy *is* a historically proven and viable concept. Philosophers like Plato and Aristotle studied and wrote while living in exactly that civilization, year in, year out. When they put down their work and walked out their door, mass participatory democracy was the world they walked into. It was an ideal perhaps, but an ideal made real.

And while you may not know it, you are also (no matter how old you are) a child of ideals turned into reality, of things that were once said to be impossible, dangerous and radical turned quotidienne.

How many mansions, for example, are now public museums, schools and hospitals?

How would their former owners react if you could travel back in time and tell them that someday their meticulously kept mansion would serve as a kinder-garten for the peasant children? For free? That their beautiful palace would be chock full of sick patients: black people, white people, Asian people, transgender people, poor people, rich people, all getting the same medical treatment?

Chances are they'd laugh themselves silly and call you a naive fool.

But the people who made that all happen were *not* naive.

At all.

And neither am I.

Democracy is not just possible. It is inevitable.

And it requires only one thing of you: that you don't give up and fall for the dismal yet somehow comforting narrative that humankind is hopeless.

So don't believe the anti-democrats' stretched-out lies. Don't be intimidated by their fear-mongering claims that the sky is going to fall down without them. And don't believe for a second that their dystopian dismal version of the future is your only choice or that 'other people' are your enemies, or that you are too stupid or incapable to handle this.

They're not, and you're not.

Anti-democrats can feel the end is nigh, which is why they're slapping on the fear and doubt thick, but their haste has made them sloppy. So many loose ends, unsubstantiated claims, dangling innuendos. Stripped of their fan club chorus of adoring journalists, they're exposed for what they are – a grasping, sorry, desperate fraud, offering nothing but hysteria and oppression. A narcissistic doctrine hidden behind a veneer of pompous righteousness.

Don't fall for it.

Notes

Introduction: Why This? Why Me? Why Now?

1 Daniel A. Bell, *The China Model: Political Meritocracy and the Limits of Democracy* (Princeton University Press 2015).

2 Christopher H. Achen & Larry M. Bartels, *Democracy for Realists: Why Elections Do Not Produce Responsive Government* (Princeton University Press 2016); Jonathan Rauch & Benjamin Wittes, 'More professionalism, less populism: how voting makes us stupid and what to do about it', Center for Effective Public Management at Brookings (May 2017), https://www.brookings.edu/wp-content/uploads/2017/05/more-professionalism-less-populism.pdf.

3 Jason Brennan, *Against Democracy* (Princeton University Press 2016); Ilya Somin, *Democracy and Political Ignorance: Why Smaller Government is Better*, 2nd edn (Stanford University Press 2016); Bryan Caplan, *The Myth of the Rational Voter: Why Democracies Choose Bad Policies* (Princeton University Press 2007).

4 Brennan, *Against Democracy*.

5 Achen & Bartels, *Democracy for Realists*.

6 Julian Baggini, 'Think democracy means the people are always right? Wrong', *Guardian* (5 October 2016), https://www.theguardian.com/commentisfree/2016/oct/05/democracy-politicians-populism-institutions.

7 Michael Sauga, 'Brexit vote underscores limits of direct democracy', *Spiegel Online* (5 July 2016), http://www.spiegel.de/international/europe/brexit-editorial-the-trouble-with-plebiscites-a-1101235.html.

8 Geoffrey Robertson, 'How to stop Brexit: get your MP to vote it down', *Guardian* (27 June 2016), https://www.theguardian.com/commentisfree/2016/jun/27/stop-brexit-mp-vote-referendum-members-parliament-act-europe.

9 Emily Badger, 'Brexit reminds us some things are too important to be left to the people', *Independent* (27 June 2017), https://www.independent.co.uk/news/uk/politics/brexit-eu-referendum-result-latest-news-democracy-vote-consequences-a7105481.html.

10 Tess Finch-Lees 'Brexit is not the high point of democracy – it's the greatest fraud ever perpetrated in British politics', *Independent* (2 February 2017), https://www.independent.co.uk/voices/brexit-referendum-alternative-facts-brexit-bill-white-paper-european-union-a7558886.html.

11 Mai'a K. Davis Cross, 'Don't be fooled by the UK election: there's nothing democratic about Brexit', *Washington Post* (7 June 2017), https://www.washingtonpost.com/news/democracy-post/wp/2017/06/07/dont-be-fooled-by-the-u-k-election-theres-nothing-democratic-about-brexit.

12 Gerard Delanty, 'Brexit and the great pretence of democracy', Routledge Blog, https://www.routledge.com/sociology/posts/10930.

13 James Traub, 'It's time for the elites to rise up against the ignorant masses', *Foreign Policy* (28 June 2016), https://

foreignpolicy.com/2016/06/28/its-time-for-the-elites-to-rise-up-against-ignorant-masses-trump-2016-brexit/.

14 David van Reybrouck, 'Why elections are bad for democracy', *Guardian* (29 June 2016), https://www.theguardian.com/politics/2016/jun/29/why-elections-are-bad-for-democracy.

15 Richard Askwith, 'People power: if we want to defend our democracy we must expel the Lords and replace them with the people', *Independent* (19 February 2018), https://www.independent.co.uk/news/long_reads/house-of-lords-abolish-people-power-reform-peoples-chamber-peers-a8197216.html.

16 Simon Wren-Lewis, 'Brexit and democracy', *Social Europe* (11 August 2017), www.socialeurope.eu/brexit-and-democracy.

17 Rauch & Wittes, 'More professionalism, less populism'.

18 Kenneth Rogoff, 'Britain's democratic failure', *Boston Globe* (24 June 2016), https://www.bostonglobe.com/opinion/2016/06/24/britain-democratic-failure/Mx888Cle7t6OUyuWyX8n2M/story.html.

19 Daniel W. Drezner, 'Yes, there is such a thing as too much democracy', *Washington Post* (28 June 2016), https://www.washingtonpost.com/posteverything/wp/2016/06/28/regarding-brexit-democracy-and-elitism.

20 Achen & Bartels, *Democracy for Realists*.

21 Sean Illing 'Two eminent political scientists: the problem with democracy is voters', *Vox* (24 June 2017), https://www.vox.com/policy-and-politics/2017/6/1/15515820/donald-trump-democracy-brexit-2016-election-europe.

22 Caleb Crain, 'The case against democracy', *New Yorker* (7 November 2016), https://www.newyorker.com/magazine/2016/11/07/the-case-against-democracy.

23 Ilya Somin, 'Democracy vs. epistocracy', *Washington Post* (3 September 2016), https://www.washingtonpost.

com/news/volokh-conspiracy/wp/2016/09/03/democ racy-vs-epistacracy.

24 Jason Brennan, 'Is this the end of democracy?', *New Statesman* (21 December 2016), https://www. newstatesman.com/politics/uk/2016/12/end-democracy; 'The right to vote should be restricted to those with knowledge', *Aeon* (29 September 2016), https://aeon.co/ ideas/the-right-to-vote-should-be-restricted-to-those-wi th-knowledge.

25 Jason Brennan, 'Can epistocracy, or knowledge-based voting, fix democracy?', *Los Angeles Times* (28 August 2016) http://www.latimes.com/opinion/op-ed/la-oe-bre nnan-epistocracy-20160828-snap-story.html.

26 E.g., Ilya Somin, 'Time to start taking voter ignorance seriously', *Washington Post* (8 November 2016), https:// www.washingtonpost.com/news/volokh-conspiracy/wp /2016/11/08/time-to-take-political-ignorance-seriously; 'Moving vans more powerful than ballot boxes', *USA Today* (18 October 2016), https://eu.usatoday.com/ story/opinion/2016/10/18/mobility-zoning-licensing-voting-minorities-column/91990486/; Bryan Caplan, '5 myths about our ballot-box behaviour', *Washington Post* (6 January 2008), http://www.washingtonpost. com/wp-dyn/content/article/2008/01/03/AR2008010 303094.html; Caplan's book was also reviewed in the *New Yorker*: Louis Menand, 'Fractured franchise' (9 July 2007), https://www.newyorker.com/magazine/ 2007/07/09/fractured-franchise; and in the *Financial Times*: Samuel Brittan 'The devil in democracy' (28 July 2007), https://www.ft.com/content/e0341766-397e-11 dc-ab48-0000779fd2ac.

27 Somin, *Democracy and Political Ignorance*.

28 Caplan, *The Myth of the Rational Voter*.

29 James Kirchick, 'The British election is a reminder of the perils of too much democracy', *Los Angeles Times*

(9 June 2017), http://www.latimes.com/opinion/op-ed/
la-oe-kirchick-uk-election-20170609-story.html.

30 Andrew Sullivan, 'Democracies end when they are too
democratic', *New York Magazine* (1 May 2016), http://
nymag.com/daily/intelligencer/2016/04/america-tyrann
y-donald-trump.html.

31 Justin Fox, 'Voters are making a mess of democracy',
Bloomberg (6 July 2016), https://www.bloomberg.com/
view/articles/2016-07-06/voters-are-making-a-mess-of-
democracy.

32 Bret Stephens, 'The year of voting recklessly', *New York
Times* (9 June 2017), https://www.nytimes.com/2017/
06/09/opinion/the-year-of-voting-recklessly.html.

**Part I: The Terrible Truth, People Aren't All that Stupid
or Evil**

1 https://twitter.com/bengoldacre/status/9648642999350
72256.

2 James Traub, 'It's time for the elites to rise up against the
ignorant masses', *Foreign Policy* (28 June 2016), https://
foreignpolicy.com/2016/06/28/its-time-for-the-elites-to-
rise-up-against-ignorant-masses-trump-2016-brexit/.

3 Josh Gabbatiss 'Brexit strongly linked to xenophobia
scientists conclude', *Independent* (27 November 2017),
https://www.independent.co.uk/news/science/brexit-pre
judice-scientists-link-foreigners-immigrants-racism-xen
ophobia-leave-eu-a8078586.html.

4 'Sir Vince Cable denies branding older Brexit voters
racist', *BBC News* (12 March 2018), https://www.bbc.
com/news/uk-politics-43367204.

5 Jonathan Chait, 'Here's the real reason everybody
thought Trump would lose', *New York Magazine* (11
May 2016), http://nymag.com/daily/intelligencer/2016/
05/heres-the-real-reason-we-all-underrated-trump.html.

6 Jeet Heer, 'Are Donald Trump's supporters idiots?', *New Republic*, https://newrepublic.com/minutes/133 447/donald-trumps-supporters-idiots; Elizabeth Zwirz, 'MSNBC's Joe Scarborough slams Trump and supporters as "openly racist"', *Fox News* (22 June 2018), http://www.foxnews.com/politics/2018/06/22/msnbcs-joe-sca rborough-slams-trump-and-supporters-as-openly-racist. html.

7 Susan Bordo, 'The destruction of Hillary Clinton: Sexism, Sanders and the millennial feminists', *Guardian* (3 April 2017), https://www.theguardian.com/us-news/commen tisfree/2017/apr/03/the-destruction-of-hillary-clinton-sexism-sanders-and-the-millennial-feminists; Rebecca Onion, 'Bad news: we're sexist', *Slate* (7 June 2017), http://www.slate.com/articles/double_x/doublex/2017/06/new_research_on_role_of_sexism_in_2016_election. html; Suzannah Weiss, 'Hillary Clinton thinks women voted against her because of 'fathers and husbands and boyfriends and male employers', *Glamour* (14 September 2017), https://www.glamour.com/story/hillary-clinton-thinks-women-voted-against-her-because-of-men.

8 Christopher H. Achen & Larry M. Bartels, *Democracy for Realists: Why Elections Do Not Produce Responsive Government* (Princeton University Press 2016), pp. 336 et seq.

9 Christopher H. Achen & Larry M. Bartels, 'Do Sanders supporters favor his policies?', *New York Times* (23 May 2016), https://www.nytimes.com/2016/05/23/opi nion/campaign-stops/do-sanders-supporters-favor-his-policies.html.

10 Ronald Brownstein, 'The great democratic age gap', *Atlantic* (2 February 2016), https://www.theatlantic. com/politics/archive/2016/02/the-great-democratic-age-gap/459570/; Stanley Feldman & Melissa Herrman, '2016 Iowa caucuses: two races decided by very different

factors', *CBS News* (2 February 2016), https://www.cbsnews.com/news/2016-iowa-caucuses-cbs-entrance-polling-analysis/.

11 Elizabeth Bruenig, 'Bernie Sanders won New Hampshire's young female vote by a landslide', *New Republic*, https://newrepublic.com/minutes/129544/bernie-sanders-won-new-hampshires-young-female-vote-landslide; 'New Hampshire primary exit poll analysis: how Trump and Sanders won', *ABC News* (9 February 2016), https://abcnews.go.com/PollingUnit/voted-live-hampshire-prim ary-exit-poll-analysis/story?id=36805930.

12 Maeve Reston, 'Hillary Clinton splits younger, older democratic women', *CNN* (10 June 2016), https://edi tion.cnn.com/2016/06/10/politics/hillary-clinton-wom en-generational-divide/index.html.

13 Farai Chideya, 'Unlike their parents, black millennials aren't a lock for Clinton', *FiveThirtyEight* (20 September 2016), https://fivethirtyeight.com/features/black-millennials-arent-united-behind-clinton-like-the ir-elders/.

14 Perry Bacon Jr. 'Huge split between older and younger blacks in the Democratic primary', *NBC News* (28 May 2016).

15 Jorge Rivas, 'Hillary Clinton won big in California's heaviest Latino districts', *Splinter News* (8 June 2016), https://splinternews.com/hillary-clinton-won-big-in-cali fornias-heaviest-latino-1793857361.

16 Ed Kilgore, 'Asian-Americans like Clinton, don't like Trump', *New York Magazine* (23 May 2016), http://nymag.com/daily/intelligencer/2016/05/asian-americans -like-clinton-dont-like-trump.html.

17 Whet Moser, 'Hillary Clinton's youth problem is also a white problem', *Chicago Magazine* (14 July 2016), http://www.chicagomag.com/city-life/July-2016/Hillary-Clintons-Youth-Problem-Is-Also-a-White-Problem/.

18 See e.g. Chideya, 'Unlike their parents, black millennials aren't a lock for Clinton'.

19 Gloria Steinem on Real Time with Bill Maher, *HBO* (5 February 2016), https://www.youtube.com/watc h?v=HoV3UgQBvh4; Alan Rappeport, 'Gloria Steinem and Madeleine Albright rebuke young women backing Bernie Sanders', *New York Times* (7 February 2016), https://www.nytimes.com/2016/02/08/us/politics/glori a-steinem-madeleine-albright-hillary-clinton-bernie-san ders.html.

20 'Vote choice', GenForward (2016), Black Youth Project & AP-NORC (University of Chicago), http://genfor wardsurvey.com/assets/uploads/2016/10/GenForward October2016FactSheetsFinal_Vote-Choice.pdf.

21 Jens Manuel Krogstad & Mark Hugo Lopez, 'Black voter turnout fell in 2016 even as record number of Americans cast ballots', *Pew Research Center* (12 May 2017), http://www.pewresearch.org/fact-tank/2017/05/ 12/black-voter-turnout-fell-in-2016-even-as-a-record-n umber-of-americans-cast-ballots/.

22 'Vote choice', GenForward.

23 Krogstad & Lopez, 'Black voter turnout fell in 2016'.

24 Gary Younge, '"Trump hasn't just done a good job, he's done a great job": the view from Muncie, Indiana', *Guardian* (22 January 2018), https://amp.theguardian. com/us-news/2018/jan/22/trump-great-job-muncie-ind iana-year-election.

25 John McCormick, 'Trump beats Clinton among least educated whites in Bloomberg poll', *Bloomberg* (8 September 2016), https://www.bloomberg.com/news/ articles/2016-09-08/trump-beats-clinton-least-educated-whites.

26 'Exit Polls', *CNN* (23 November 2016), https://edition. cnn.com/election/2016/results/exit-polls/national/presi dent.

27 'Cut migration to 1950s level says Nigel Farage', *Daily Express* (31 March 2015), https://www.express.co.uk/news/politics/567577/Ukip-Nigel-Farage-wants-limit-migrants-30-000.

28 Katie Hopkins, 'Rescue boats? I'd use gunships to stop migrants', *The Sun* (17 April 2015).

29 www.change.org/p-/l-b-c-we-the-people-support-of-katie-hopkins (2018 – since removed).

30 Harley Tamplin, 'People didn't vote for Brexit because they are racist, study finds', *Metro UK* (21 December 2017), http://metro.co.uk/2017/12/21/people-didnt-vote-brexit-racist-study-finds-7176198/.

31 Kully-Kaur Ballagan & Glenn Gottfried, 'Attitudes to immigration have softened since referendum but most still want to see it reduced', *Ipsos Mori* (26 March 2018), https://www.ipsos.com/ipsos-mori/en-uk/attitudes-immigration-have-softened-referendum-most-still-want-see-it-reduced.

32 Kully-Kaur Ballagan & Glenn Gottfried, 'New global study reveals unease about immigration around the world', *Ipsos Mori* (14 September 2017), https://www.ipsos.com/ipsos-mori/en-uk/new-global-study-reveals-unease-about-immigration-around-world.

33 Ballagan & Gottfried, 'Attitudes to immigration have softened since referendum'; another survey conducted by an organization dedicated to acting in the remembrance of the Armenian genocide came to similar results: May Bulman, 'British people becoming more sympathetic towards refugees and immigrants, survey suggests', *Independent* (10 May 2018), https://www.independent.co.uk/news/uk/home-news/uk-refugees-immigration-sympathy-kind-survey-brexit-a8344841.html.

34 Dreda Say Mitchell, 'If May betrays us on migration, minority Brexit voters will switch sides', *Guardian*

(26 January 2017), https://www.theguardian.com/commentisfree/2017/jan/26/if-may-betrays-us-on-migration-minority-ethnic-brexiters-will-switch-sides; Nazia Parveen, 'Why do some ethnic minority voters want to leave the EU?', *Guardian* (1 June 2016), https://www.theguardian.com/politics/2016/jun/01/british-asians-views-eu-referendum-figures-brexit.

35 Dreda Say Mitchell, 'Of course UKIP plays the race card, but I'm still voting for Brexit', *Guardian* (22 June 2018), https://www.theguardian.com/commentisfree/2016/jun/22/remain-may-win-eu-referendum-but-labour-party-loser; Iman Amrani, 'Why do some of us with migrant parents want to vote for Brexit?', *Guardian* (22 June 2016), https://www.theguardian.com/commentisfree/2016/jun/22/migrant-parents-vote-brexit-british-vote-leave.

36 Alex Wessely, 'The Mau Mau case five years on', *Leigh Day* (6 October 2017), https://www.leighday.co.uk/Blog/October-2017/Kenyan-colonial-abuses-apology-five-years-on; Owen Bowcott, 'Mau Mau lawsuit due to begin at High Court', *Guardian* (22 May 2016), https://www.theguardian.com/law/2016/may/22/mau-mau-kenya-compensation-lawsuit-high-court; Sandeep Gopalan & Roslyn Fuller, 'Enforcing international law: states, IOs and courts as shaming reference groups', 39(1) *Brooklyn Journal of International Law* (2014), pp. 73–158, at 134 et seq.

37 Encyclopaedia Britannica, 'Ku Klux Klan' (25 May 2018); 'Ku Klux Klan', Southern Poverty Law Center, https://www.splcenter.org/fighting-hate/extremist-files/ideology/ku-klux-klan.

38 Rebecca Woods, 'England in 1966: racism and ignorance in the Midlands', *BBC* (1 June 2016), http://www.bbc.com/news/uk-england-birmingham-36388761; 'Letters: Sign of the times of racism in England that was all too

familiar', *Guardian* (22 October 2015), https://www.theguardian.com/world/2015/oct/22/sign-of-the-times-of-racism-in-england-that-was-all-too-familiar.

39 Sarah A. Ogilvie & Scott Miller, *Refuge Denied: The St. Louis Passengers and the Holocaust* (University of Wisconsin Press 2006), esp. p. 24.

40 Daniel A. Bell, *The China Model: Political Meritocracy and the Limits of Democracy* (Princeton University Press 2015), p. 24.

41 Ilya Somin, *Democracy and Political Ignorance: Why Smaller Government is Better*, 2nd edn (Stanford University Press 2016), p. 19.

42 Somin, *Democracy and Political Ignorance*, p. 20; Jason Brennan, *Against Democracy* (Princeton University Press 2016), p. 29.

43 Brennan, *Against Democracy*, pp. 25 et seq.

44 Bryan Caplan, *The Myth of the Rational Voter: Why Democracies Choose Bad Policies* (Princeton University Press 2007), l. 1740.

45 Achen & Bartels, *Democracy for Realists*, p. 36.

46 Gerard Delanty, 'Brexit and the great pretence of democracy', Routledge Blog, https://www.routledge.com/sociology/posts/10930.

47 Steven Sloman & Philip Fernbach, *The Knowledge Illusion: Why We Never Think Alone* (Penguin 2017), pp. 91–104.

48 Sloman & Fernbach, *The Knowledge Illusion*, p. 5.

49 Sloman & Fernbach, *The Knowledge Illusion*, p. 13.

50 Sloman & Fernbach, *The Knowledge Illusion*, p. 120.

51 Sloman & Fernbach, *The Knowledge Illusion*, p. 120.

52 Arthur Lupia & Markus Prior, 'Money, time and political knowledge: distinguishing quick recall and political learning skills', 52 *American Journal of Political Science* (2008), pp. 16–183.

53 John Mark Hansen, 'Individuals, institutions and public

preferences over public finance', 92 *American Political Science Review* (1998), pp. 513–531.

54 Hansen, 'Individuals, institutions and public preferences over public finance', p. 518.

55 Achen & Bartels, *Democracy for Realists*, p. 295.

56 Achen & Bartels, *Democracy for Realists*, p. 295.

57 Caplan, *The Myth of the Rational Voter*, ll. 1705, 2792; Somin, *Democracy and Political Ignorance*, pp. 5, 75; Bell, *The China Model*, p. 24; Brennan, *Against Democracy*, p. 31 (who connects this 'rational ignorance' point more to pure knowledge than to judgement).

58 Douglas Adams, *The Restaurant at the End of the Universe* (Pan 1980), pp. 252 et seq.

59 For more on gerrymandering and vote-discounting, see Roslyn Fuller, *Beasts and Gods: How Democracy Changed Its Meaning and Lost Its Purpose* (Zed Books 2015), pp. 43 et seq.

60 Caplan, *The Myth of the Rational Voter*, l. 323.

61 Caplan, *The Myth of the Rational Voter*, l. 707.

62 'Eight of world's biggest banks to settle cartel case with Brussels', *Irish Times* (19 November 2017), https://www.irishtimes.com/business/financial-services/eight-of-world-s-biggest-banks-to-settle-cartel-case-with-brussels-1.3297713.

63 Philip Ryan, 'Watchdog examines cartel allegations among waste companies in Dublin', *Irish Independent* (21 January 2018), https://www.independent.ie/irish-news/watchdog-examines-cartel-allegations-among-waste-companies-in-dublin-36512204.html; New York City's garbage was collected by a mafia-run cartel for 40 years: Allen R. Myerson, 'The garbage wars: cracking the cartel', *New York Times* (1995), https://www.nytimes.com/1995/07/30/business/the-garbage-wars-cracking-the-cartel.html.

64 John Pecman, Commissioner of Competition, 'Shining a

light into the shadows: what price fixing investigations tells Canadians', *Competition Bureau of Canada* (5 February 2018), http://www.competitionbureau.gc.ca/eic/site/cb-bc.nsf/eng/04335.html; Andrew Russel, '7 Canadian companies committed indictable offenses in bread-price fixing scandal: competition bureau', *Global News* (31 January 2018), https://globalnews.ca/news/3998023/bread-price-fixing-scandal-competition-act-crimes/.

65 Bryan Caplan & Tyler Cowen, 'Do we underestimate the benefits of cultural competition?', 94(2) *American Economic Review* (2004), pp. 402–407.

66 Daniel Klein, *What Do Economists Contribute?* (New York University Press 1999).

67 Andrei Shleifer 'State vs private ownership', 12(4) *Journal of Economic Perspectives* (1998), pp. 133–150.

68 Steven Rhoads, *The Economist's View of the World: Government, Markets and Public Policy* (Cambridge University Press 1985).

69 Paul Rubin, 'Folk Economics', 70(1) *Southern Economic Journal* (2003), pp. 157–171.

70 Caplan, *The Myth of the Rational Voter*, l. 741.

71 Caplan, *The Myth of the Rational Voter*, l. 792.

72 Caplan, *The Myth of the Rational Voter*, ll. 792 et seq.

73 See, e.g., Susan Sell & Aseem Prakash, 'Using ideas strategically: the contest between business and NGO networks in intellectual property rights', 48(1) *International Studies Quarterly* (2004), p. 143; Roslyn Fuller, 'Enclosing the democratic commons: private organizations and the legislative process', Conference Paper (ASSA, 2015).

74 Caplan, *The Myth of the Rational Voter*, ll. 2914, 2930.

75 Caplan, *The Myth of the Rational Voter*, ll. 1210 et seq., 1673.

76 Bryan Caplan, 'Overruling the majority', *Cato Unbound*

(19 November 2006), https://www.cato-unbound.org/2006/11/19/bryan-caplan/overruling-majority.

77 Achen & Bartels, *Democracy for Realists*, p. 76.
78 Achen & Bartels, *Democracy for Realists*, p. 139.
79 Jeff Tessin, 'Representation and government performance', PhD dissertation, Department of Politics, Princeton (2008), http://citation.allacademic.com//meta/p_mla_apa_research_citation/2/6/6/4/4/pages266445/p266445-3.php, p. 6.
80 Tessin, 'Representation and government performance', p. 18.
81 Tessin, 'Representation and government performance', p. 16.
82 Phil Kadner, 'Let's understand why Illinois has the highest property taxes', *Chicago Sun Times* (1 June 2017), https://chicago.suntimes.com/columnists/lets-understand-why-illinois-has-the-highest-property-taxes/.
83 Actually, these are the values I obtained by spending some time between Illinois real estate sites and an online tax calculator (https://smartasset.com/taxes/illinois-property-tax-calculator); other sources suggest property tax bills as high as $10k a year in some areas; see Sarah Schulte, 'Some Chicago Homeowners Seeing Big Increase in Property Tax Assessments', *ABC 7 Eyewitness News* (21 May 2018), https://abc7chicago.com/realestate/some-chicago-homeowners-seeing-big-increase-in-property-ty-tax-assessments/3504190/.
84 Tessin, 'Representation and government performance', p. 25.
85 Jordyn Reiland, 'Crystal Lake majority oppose library referendum', *Northwest Herald* (9 November 2016), https://www.nwherald.com/2016/11/08/crystal-lake-majority-oppose-library-referendum/a1yv8ix/.
86 Kurt Snibbe, 'Proposition 13: on its 40th anniversary,

we look back at its history and what's new', *Mercury News* (7 June 2018), https://www.mercurynews.com/2018/06/07/proposition-13-on-its-40th-anniversary-we-look-at-its-history-and-whats-new-2/.

87 Shaun Bowler & Todd Donovan, *Demanding Choices: Opinion, Voting and Direct Democracy* (University of Michigan, 1998), pp. 2 et seq.

88 Bowler & Donovan, *Demanding Choices*, p. 91.

89 Snibbe, 'Proposition 13'.

90 Snibbe, 'Proposition 13'.

91 Ester Bloom, 'Canadians may pay more taxes than Americans, but here's what they get for their money', *CNBC* (7 August 2017), https://www.cnbc.com/2017/08/07/canadians-may-pay-more-taxes-than-americans-but-theres-a-catch.html.

92 'The East Bay Hills fire, Oakland-Berkeley, California', US Fire Administration/Technical Report Series, FEMA, USFA-TR-060/October 1991, p. 45.

93 'The East Bay Hills fire', pp. 19 et seq.

94 'US Census 1990, California, population and housing unit counts', p. 2, https://www.census.gov/prod/cen1990/cph2/cph-2-6.pdf.

95 See, e.g., Bell, *The China Model*, p. 28; also Sloman & Fernbach, *The Knowledge Illusion*, p. 190.

96 Achen & Bartels, *Democracy for Realists*, p. 84.

97 Achen & Bartels, *Democracy for Realists*, pp. 116 et seq., 147.

98 Anthony Fowler & Andrew B. Hall, 'Do shark attacks influence presidential elections? Reassessing a prominent finding on voter competence' (30 January 2017), http://www.andrewbenjaminhall.com/FowlerHall_Sharks.pdf, p. 2.

99 Jonathan Rauch & Benjamin Wittes, 'More professionalism, less populism: how voting makes us stupid

and what to do about it', Center for Effective Public Management at Brookings (May 2017), https://www.brookings.edu/wp-content/uploads/2017/05/more-professionalism-less-populism.pdf.

100 Michael Hotchkiss, 'Achen challenges popular conceptions of American democracy', Princeton University (2 June 2016), https://www.princeton.edu/news/2016/06/06/achen-challenges-popular-conceptions-american-democracy.

101 E.g., Celia Paris, 'Review of *Democracy for Realists*', 25(1) *The Good Society* (2016), pp. 119–127.

102 Andy Sullivan, 'It's not just the economy: why football and sharks can affect elections', *Reuters* (6 October 2012), https://www.reuters.com/article/us-usa-campaign-uninformed-voters/its-not-just-the-economy-why-football-and-sharks-can-affect-elections-idUSBRE8950372012106.

103 Megan Gambino, 'The shark attacks that were the inspiration for *Jaws*', *Smithsonian.com* (6 August 2012), https://www.smithsonianmag.com/history/the-shark-attacks-that-were-the-inspiration-for-jaws-15220260.

104 Christopher H. Achen & Larry M. Bartels, 'Blind retrospection: why shark attacks are bad for democracy', Center for the Study of Democratic Institutions, Vanderbilt University, Working Paper 5-2013 (2012), https://www.vanderbilt.edu/csdi/research/CSDI_WP_05-2013.pdf (citing Michael Capuzzo, *Close to Shore: A True Story of Terror in an Age of Innocence* (Broadway Books 2001), p. 274; and Richard G. Fernicola *Twelve Days of Terror: A Definitive Investigation of the 1916 New Jersey Shark Attacks* (Lyons Press 2001), p. 174).

105 Gambino, 'The shark attacks that were the inspiration for *Jaws*'.

106 Brian Maye, 'An Irishman's diary about the shark attacks that inspired *Jaws*', *Irish Times* (23 July 2016).

107 Achen & Bartels, *Democracy for Realists*, pp. 116 et seq.

108 Achen & Bartels, *Democracy for Realists*, pp. 127 et seq.

109 Achen & Bartels, 'Blind retrospection', fn. 18.

110 Achen & Bartels, 'Blind retrospection', p. 16.

111 Christopher H. Achen & Larry M. Bartels, 'Statistics as if politics mattered: a reply to Fowler and Hall', *Journal of Politics* (July 2018).

112 Manual of the Legislature of New Jersey, 1909, 1913, 1917 and 1921 (Gazette Publishing Co., Trenton, New Jersey).

113 Fowler & Hall, 'Do shark attacks influence presidential elections?', pp. 6 et seq.

114 Fowler & Hall, 'Do shark attacks influence presidential elections?', p. 1.

115 Fowler & Hall, 'Do shark attacks influence presidential elections?', p. 1.

116 Fowler & Hall, 'Do shark attacks influence presidential elections?', pp. 8 et seq.

117 Fowler & Hall, 'Do shark attacks influence presidential elections?', p. 15.

118 Achen & Bartels, 'Blind retrospection', p. 10.

119 Fowler & Hall, 'Do shark attacks influence presidential elections?', pp. 16 et seq.

120 Fowler & Hall, 'Do shark attacks influence presidential elections?', pp. 16 et seq.

121 Achen & Bartels, 'Blind retrospection', p. 9 (emphasis added).

122 Christopher H. Achen & Larry M. Bartels, 'Government for the people: a reply to the symposium', *Critical Review* (September 2018).

123 See Susan Stokes, 'Accountability for realists', *Critical Review* (11 June 2018).

124 Achen & Bartels, *Democracy for Realists*, pp. 130 et seq.

125 Achen & Bartels, *Democracy for Realists*, pp. 134 et seq.

126 Achen & Bartels, *Democracy for Realists*, p. 144.

127 Achen & Bartels, *Democracy for Realists*, p. 211.

128 Peter Carroll, 'Book review: *Democracy for Realists: Why Elections Do Not Produce Responsive Government* by Christopher H. Achen and Larry M. Bartels', *London School of Economics Blog*, http://blogs.lse.ac.uk/lsereviewofbooks/2017/01/30/book-review-democracy-for-realists-why-elections-do-not-produce-responsive-government-by-christopher-h-achen-and-larry-m-bartels/. The almost sole voice against this trend was Andrew Gelman, 'Do shark attacks swing elections?', *Washington Post* (28 October 2016), https://www.washingtonpost.com/news/monkey-cage/wp/2016/10/28/do-shark-attacks-swing-elections.

129 Antje Schwennicke, Elizabeth F. Cohen, Neil Roberts, Andrew Sabl, Isabela Mares & Gerald C. Wright, 'A discussion of Christopher H. Achen and Larry M. Bartels, *Democracy for Realists: Why Elections Do Not Produce Responsive Government*', 15(1) *Perspectives on Politics* (2017), pp. 148–162.

130 It took until mid-2018 for mild criticism of *Democracy for Realists* to surface; see, e.g., Stokes, 'Accountability for realists'; Simone Chambers, 'Human life is group life'; and William A. Galston, 'Getting real about realism: voters are more reasonable and democracies more responsive than Achen and Bartels would suggest' – all in *Critical Review* (2018).

131 Achen and Bartels, 'Government for the people: a reply to the symposium'.

132 Achen & Bartels, *Democracy for Realists*, p. 9 (emphasis added).

133 Rauch & Wittes, 'More professionalism, less populism' (emphasis added).

134 Somin, *Democracy and Political Ignorance*, p. 71.

135 Brennan, *Against Democracy*, p. 3.

136 Dylan Matthews, 'Remember that study saying America is an oligarchy? 3 rebuttals say it's wrong', *Vox* (9 May 2016), https://www.vox.com/2016/5/9/11502464/gilens-page-oligarchy-study.

137 Keith E. Stanovich, 'Were Trump voters irrational?', *Quillette* (28 September 2017), http://quillette.com/2017/09/28/trump-voters-irrational/.

138 For a good summary, see Maria Konnikova, 'Is social psychology biased against Republicans?', *New Yorker* (30 October 2014), https://www.newyorker.com/science/maria-konnikova/social-psychology-biased-republicans.

139 Charles S. Faber & Milton R. Lodge, 'Motivated skepticism in the evaluation of political beliefs', 50 *American Journal of Political Science* (2006), pp. 755–769; Richard F. West, Russell J. Meserve & Keith Stanovich, 'Cognitive sophistication does not attenuate the bias blind spot', 103(3) *Journal of Personality and Social Psychology* (2012), pp. 506–519; Achen & Bartels, *Democracy for Realists*, p. 310 (the latter only go so far as to admit that intellectuals are as bad as everyone else).

140 Mai'a K. Davis Cross, 'Don't be fooled by the UK election: there's nothing democratic about Brexit', *Washington Post* (7 June 2017), https://www.washingtonpost.com/news/democracy-post/wp/2017/06/07/dont-be-fooled-by-the-u-k-election-theres-nothing-democratic-about-brexit.

141 Kenneth Rogoff, quoted in Amanda Taub & Max

Fisher, 'Why referendums aren't as democratic as they seem', *New York Times* (4 October 2016), https://www.nytimes.com/2016/10/05/world/americas/colombia-brexit-referendum-farc-cameron-santos.html.

Part II: Fixing Politics the Anti-Democrat Way

1 Jason Brennan, *Against Democracy* (Princeton University Press 2016), p. 140.
2 Brennan, *Against Democracy*, p. 15.
3 Brennan, *Against Democracy*, p. 121.
4 Brennan, *Against Democracy*, p. 169.
5 Brennan, *Against Democracy*, p. 132.
6 Brennan, *Against Democracy*, p. 116.
7 Brennan, *Against Democracy*, p. 133.
8 Brennan, *Against Democracy*, p. 129.
9 Brennan, *Against Democracy*, p. 142.
10 Brennan, *Against Democracy*, p. 144.
11 Brennan, *Against Democracy*, p. 172.
12 Bryan Caplan, *The Myth of the Rational Voter: Why Democracies Choose Bad Policies* (Princeton University Press 2007), l. 3727.
13 Caplan, *The Myth of the Rational Voter*, l. 3761.
14 Caplan, *The Myth of the Rational Voter*, l. 3770.
15 'I am part of the resistance inside the Trump administration', *New York Times* (5 September 2018), https://www.nytimes.com/2018/09/05/opinion/trump-white-house-anonymous-resistance.html.
16 Caplan, *The Myth of the Rational Voter*, l. 3257.
17 Military and Paramilitary Activities in and Against Nicaragua (*Nicaragua vs United States of America*) Merits, Judgement, ICJ Reports 1986.
18 Ilya Somin, *Democracy and Political Ignorance: Why Smaller Government is Better,* 2nd edn (Stanford University Press 2016), p. 6.

19 Somin, *Democracy and Political Ignorance*, pp. 62 et seq.

20 Somin, *Democracy and Political Ignorance*, p. 136.

21 Somin, *Democracy and Political Ignorance*, p. 161.

22 Somin, *Democracy and Political Ignorance*, pp. 189 et seq.

23 Somin, *Democracy and Political Ignorance*, p. 136.

24 Somin, *Democracy and Political Ignorance*, p. 164.

25 Somin, *Democracy and Political Ignorance*, p. 164.

26 Somin, *Democracy and Political Ignorance*, pp. 147 et seq.

27 Somin, *Democracy and Political Ignorance*, pp. 148–149 (citing Rex R. Johnson & Daniel M. Campbell, *Black Migration in America: A Social Demographic History* (Duke University Press 1981)).

28 Somin, *Democracy and Political Ignorance*, p. 151.

29 Somin, *Democracy and Political Ignorance*, p. 179.

30 Jonathan Rauch, 'How American politics went insane', *Atlantic* (July/August 2016), https://www.theatlantic.com/magazine/archive/2016/07/how-american-politics-went-insane/485570/.

31 Rauch, 'How American politics went insane'.

32 www.dictionary.com.

33 Rauch, 'How American politics went insane'.

34 Rauch, 'How American politics went insane'.

35 Jonathan Rauch & Benjamin Wittes, 'More professionalism, less populism: how voting makes us stupid and what to do about it' (May 2017, Center for Effective Public Management at Brookings) https://www.brookings.edu/wp-content/uploads/2017/05/more-professionalism-less-populism.pdf.

36 Rauch & Wittes, 'More professionalism, less populism'.

37 Rauch & Wittes, 'More professionalism, less populism'.

38 Rauch, 'How American politics went insane'.

39 Rauch, 'How American politics went insane'.

40 Rauch & Wittes, 'More professionalism, less populism'.

41 Rauch & Wittes, 'More professionalism, less populism'.

42 Zack Whittaker, 'In Obama's final year, US secret court denied record number of surveillance requests', *Zero Day* (20 April 2017), http://www.zdnet.com/article/in-obamas-final-year-us-secret-court-denied-record-num ber-of-surveillance-requests/; Erika Eichelberger, 'FISA court has rejected .03 percent of all government surveillance requests', *Mother Jones* (10 June 2013); Jason Koebler, 'The US surveillance court hasn't turned down an NSA request this decade', *Motherboard* (1 May 2014), https://motherboard.vice.com/en_us/article/78x84a/th e-us-surveillance-court-hasnt-turned-down-an-nsa-re quest-this-decade; Evan Perez, 'Secret court's oversight gets scrutiny', *Wall Street Journal* (9 June 2013), https:// www.wsj.com/articles/SB10001424127887324904004578535670310514616.

43 Glenn Greenwald, 'FISA court oversight: a look inside a secret and empty process', *Guardian* (19 June 2013), https://www.theguardian.com/commentisfree/2013/jun/19/fisa-court-oversight-process-secrecy.

44 Daniel A. Bell, *The China Model: Political Meritocracy and the Limits of Democracy* (Princeton University Press 2015), p. 5.

45 Bell, *The China Model*, p. 80.

46 Bell, *The China Model*, pp. 89 et seq.

47 Bell, *The China Model*, p. 100.

48 Bell, *The China Model*, p. 100.

49 Bell, *The China Model*, p. 119.

50 Bell, *The China Model*, p. 118 (emphasis added).

51 Bell, *The China Model*, p. 120.

52 The figure of 10k was obtained from https://www.statista.com/statistics/278349/average-annual-salary-of -an-employee-in-china/ and converted to USD on 23 January 2018. Other sources confirm this general range.

According to Forbes, median monthly wages are $1,135 (or $13,620 annually) in Shanghai and $983 (or $11,796 annually) in Beijing: see Kenneth Rapoza, 'China wage levels equal to or surpass parts of Europe', *Forbes* (16 August 2017), https://www.forbes.com/sites/kenrapoza/2017/08/16/china-wage-levels-equal-to-or-surpass-parts-of-europe/#3d4629563e7f. Another source claims average white-collar pay checks in more than thirty major cities to be $1,100 a month (or $13,200 annually): see 'Strong demand for workers in China, so why aren't wages rising?', *South China Morning Post* (24 July 2017), https://www.scmp.com/news/china/economy/article/2103817/strong-demand-workers-china-so-why-arent-wages-rising.

53 Rapoza, 'China wage levels equal to or surpass parts of Europe'.

54 Bell, *The China Model*, p. 121. It is unclear if this is in USD or Singapore dollars, but it doesn't make much of a difference either way – as of December 2018, 1.2 million Singapore dollars were the equivalent to nearly 900k US dollars.

55 Bell, *The China Model*, p. 121.

56 Bell, *The China Model*, p. 173.

57 Bell, *The China Model*, p. 173.

58 Bell, *The China Model*, pp. 83–88.

59 Bell, *The China Model*, p. 126.

60 Bell, *The China Model*, p. 67.

61 Bell, *The China Model*, p. 173. Bell's exact words are: 'Political meritocracy has been insufficiently developed in China. The political system needs to be further "meritocratized".'

62 Bell, *The China Model*, p. 30.

63 Bell, *The China Model*, pp. 51 et seq., 162; Brennan mentions a similar mechanism in *Against Democracy*, pp. 215 et seq.

64 Bell, *The China Model*, p. 166.

65 Bell, *The China Model*, p. 196.

66 Bell, *The China Model*, p. 196.

67 Jennifer Schuessler, 'Nicolas Berggruen wants to bridge the East–West gap', *New York Times* (15 September 2015), https://www.nytimes.com/2015/09/16/arts/nicolas-berggruen-wants-to-bridge-the-east-west-gap.html; 'Advisory Board', Berggruen Institute, https://www.berggruen.org/people/daniel-bell/.

68 Nicolas Berggruen & Nathan Gardels, *Intelligent Governance for the 21st Century: A Middle Way Between West and East* (Polity 2013).

69 Berggruen & Gardels, *Intelligent Governance for the 21st Century*, pp. 51 et seq.

70 Berggruen & Gardels, *Intelligent Governance for the 21st Century*, p. 143.

71 Berggruen & Gardels, *Intelligent Governance for the 21st Century*, p. 135.

72 'Members and Advisors', Berggruen Institute, Philosophy and Culture Center, https://www.berggruen.org/people/group/members-advisors/.

73 E.g. Bell, *The China Model*, pp. ix, 118, 190; Brennan, *Against Democracy* ('The Enfranchisement Lottery'), pp. 214 et seq.; Brennan, 'Can epistocracy, or knowledge-based voting, fix democracy?' *Los Angeles Times* (28 August 2016), http://www.latimes.com/opinion/op-ed/la-oe-brennan-epistocracy-20160828-snap-story.html; Berggruen & Gardels, *Intelligent Governance for the 21st Century*, pp. 85 et seq.; Ilya Somin, 'Time to Start Taking Voter Ignorance Seriously', *Washington Post* (8 November 2016), https://www.washingtonpost.com/news/volokh-conspiracy/wp/2016/11/08/time-to-take-political-ignorance-seriously. Caplan, in *The Myth of the Rational Voter*, does not (as far as I am aware) explicitly advocate sortition, although one of his main

themes, 'Enlightened Preferences', revolves around the exact same logic – that voters would make different decisions if only they knew 'better'.

74 Nicholas Gruen, 'An Ancient Greek idea could foil Brexit's democratic tragedy', *Guardian* (16 January 2018), https://www.theguardian.com/commentisfree/2018/jan/16/democratic-tragedy-brexit-ancient-greece-citizens-assembly-democracy.

75 Gruen, 'An Ancient Greek idea could foil Brexit's democratic tragedy' (emphasis added).

76 P. J. Rhodes, 'The polis and the alternatives', in *The Cambridge Ancient History, Vol. VI, The Fourth Century BC*, 2nd edn (Cambridge University Press 1994), pp. 565–591; E. S. Staveley, *Greek and Roman Voting and Elections* (Thames and Hudson 1972), p. 84; E. M. Walker, 'The Periclean Democracy', in *The Cambridge Ancient History, Vol. V, Athens 478–401 BC* (Cambridge University Press 1927).

77 Rhodes, 'The polis and the alternatives', pp. 567 et seq.; Mogens Herman Hansen, 'Did the Athenian Ecclesia legislate after 403/2 BC?', 20 *GRBS* (1979), pp. 27–53, at 49; Mogens Herman Hansen, '*Nomos* and *Psephisma* in fourth-century Athens', in 19 *GRBS* (1978), pp. 315–330, at 328; Mogens Herman Hansen, 'Initiative and decision: the separation of powers in fourth-century Athens', 22 *GRBS* (1981), pp. 345–370, at 366; W. S. Ferguson, 'The fall of the Athenian Empire', *The Cambridge Ancient History, Vol. V, Athens 478–401 BC* (Cambridge University Press 1927), pp. 374 et seq.

78 Gruen, 'An Ancient Greek idea could foil Brexit's democratic tragedy'.

79 Robin Cohen, 'Beating the Cambridge Analyticas: change the way we (s)elect our representatives', *OpenDemocracy* (24 March 2018), https://www.open

democracy.net/uk/robin-cohen/beating-cambridge-ana
lyticas-change-way-we-select-our-representatives.

80 Paul Cartledge, *Democracy: A Life*, 2nd edn (Oxford
University Press 2018), p. 70.

81 'Statistical bulletin: public sector employment, UK:
March 2018', Office for National Statistics UK (12 June
2018), https://www.ons.gov.uk/employmentandlabour
market/peopleinwork/publicsectorpersonnel/bulletins/
publicsectoremployment/latest#civil-service-employme
nt-rises.

82 Andy Riga, 'Quebec's 1995 referendum: 140 minutes of agony', *Montreal Gazette* (30 October 2015),
https://montrealgazette.com/news/local-news/quebecs-
1995-referendum-140-minutes-of-agony.

83 'Hello divorce, goodbye De Valera, 1995', RTE Archives,
https://www.rte.ie/archives/2015/1123/748645-divorce-
referendum/; 'Ireland: "Yes" on divorce – but barely',
CNN (26 November 1995) http://edition.cnn.com/
WORLD/9511/ireland_vote/.

84 'Abortion in Ireland: legal timeline', Irish Family
Planning Association, https://www.ifpa.ie/Hot-Topics/
Abortion/Abortion-in-Ireland-Timeline.

85 'Referendum to abolish Seanad is defeated', *RTE* (5
October 2013), https://www.rte.ie/news/2013/1005/478
505-referendum-count/.

86 'EU referendum results', *BBC News*, http://www.bbc.
com/news/politics/eu_referendum/results.

87 E.g. Gruen, 'An Ancient Greek idea could foil Brexit's
democratic tragedy'; Richard Askwith, 'People power:
if we want to defend our democracy we must expel the
Lords and replace them with the people', *UK Independent*
(19 February 2018), https://www.independent.co.uk/
news/long_reads/house-of-lords-abolish-people-power-
reform-peoples-chamber-peers-a8197216.html.; David
van Reybrouck, 'Why elections are bad for democracy',

Guardian (29 June 2016), https://www.theguardian.com/politics/2016/jun/29/why-elections-are-bad-for-democracy.

88 First Report on the Convention of the Constitution (March 2013), http://www.constitutionalconvention.ie/AttachmentDownload.ashx?mid=e1f8e128-2496-e211-a5a0-005056a32ee4.

89 David Van Reybrouck, *Against Elections: The Case for Democracy* (Vintage 2016), p. 146.

90 Van Reybrouck, *Against Elections*, p. 146.

91 Roslyn Fuller, 'Enclosing the democratic commons: private organizations and the legislative process', Conference Paper (ASSA, 2015), pp. 33 et seq., 151 et seq.

92 M. I. Finley, 'Athenian demagogues', in P. J. Rhodes, ed., *Athenian Democracy* (Edinburgh University Press 2004), pp. 173 et seq.

93 See, e.g., Stephen V. Tracy, 'The wrongful execution of the Hellenotamai (Antiphon 5.69–71) and the Lapis Primus', 109(1) *Classical Philology* (2014), pp. 1–10.

94 See, e.g., Fuller, 'Enclosing the democratic commons', pp. 89 et seq.

95 Askwith, 'People power'.

96 Van Reybrouck, *Against Elections*, p. 146.

97 Breda Heffernan, 'Dublin Airport trials "honesty-based", snack fridges for passengers "in a hurry"', *Irish Independent* (5 June 2018), https://www.independent.ie/life/travel/travel-news/dublin-airport-trials-honestybased-snack-fridges-for-passengers-in-a-hurry-36979292.html.

98 Gruen, 'An Ancient Greek idea could foil Brexit's democratic tragedy'.

99 Gruen, 'An Ancient Greek idea could foil Brexit's democratic tragedy'.

100 Askwith, 'People power'.

101 Van Reybrouck, 'Why elections are bad for democracy'.

Part III   A World You Might Want to Actually Live In (Fuller Democracy)

1 Roslyn Fuller, 'Enclosing the democratic commons: private organizations and the legislative process', Conference Paper (ASSA, 2015).

2 E.g., Harry Cockburn, 'NHS privatisation soars as private companies win 70 per cent of clinical contracts in England', *Independent* (30 December 2017), https://www.independent.co.uk/news/health/nhs-privatisation-contracts-virgin-care-richard-branson-jeremy-hunt-a8134386.html; Ciarán Hancock, 'State sold Aer Lingus for €335 million – where did the money go?', *Irish Times* (14 April 2017), https://www.irishtimes.com/business/economy/state-sold-aer-lingus-stake-for-335m-where-did-the-money-go-1.3047809; Diana Hembree, 'CEO pay skyrockets to 361 times that of the average worker', *Forbes* (22 May 2018), https://www.forbes.com/sites/dianahembree/2018/05/22/ceo-pay-skyrockets-to-361-times-that-of-the-average-worker/#6a9751c5776d. On elite vs average citizen influence over legislation, see also Martin Gilens & Benjamin I. Page, 'Testing theories of American politics: elites, interest groups and average citizens', *Perspectives on Politics* (2014), p. 564.

3 Bruce Ackerman & James S. Fishkin, *Deliberation Day* (Yale University Press 2005).

4 Ackerman & Fishkin, *Deliberation Day*.

5 Tom Batchelor, 'Corbyn says Labour would consider state-owned Facebook rival', *UK Independent* (23 August 2018), https://www.independent.co.uk/news/uk/politics/jeremy-corbyn-facebook-state-owned-so

cial-media-bbc-iplayer-privacy-labour-public-owner-ship-a8504151.html.

6 Magdalena Kunkel, 'Participatory budgeting – Portuguese style', Centre for Public Impact (22 March 2018), https://www.centreforpublicimpact.org/particip atory-budgeting-portuguese-style/.

7 Yves Sintomer, Carsten Herzberg, Giovanni Allegretti, Anja Röcke & Mariana Alves, 'Participatory budgeting worldwide: updated version', Engagement Global, on behalf of the Ministry for Economic Cooperation and Development, Germany, p. 27.

8 Sintomer, Herzberg, Allegretti, Röcke & Alves, 'Participatory budgeting worldwide', p. 28.

9 Sintomer, Herzberg, Allegretti, Röcke & Alves, 'Participatory budgeting worldwide', pp. 28, 39.

10 Xenophon, *Memorabilia*, 3.7.6.

11 M. M. Markle, 'Jury pay and Assembly pay at Athens', in P. J. Rhodes, ed., *Athenian Democracy* (Edinburgh University Press 2004), pp. 95, 106; Marcus Tod, 'The economic background of the fifth century', in *The Cambridge Ancient History, Vol. V, Athens 478–401 BC* (Cambridge University Press 1927), pp. 24, 30; E. M. Walker, 'The Periclean Democracy', in *The Cambridge Ancient History, Vol. V, Athens 478–401 BC* (Cambridge University Press 1927), pp. 103, 105, 110; P. J. Rhodes, 'The polis and the alternatives', in *The Cambridge Ancient History, Vol. VI, The Fourth Century BC*, 2nd edn (Cambridge University Press 1994), pp. 565–591, at 566; E. S. Staveley, *Greek and Roman Voting and Elections* (Thames and Hudson 1972), p. 53.

12 Aristotle, *Politics*; Xenophon, *Memorabilia*, 3.7.6; Isocrates, *Areopagiticus*, 10.23–26.

13 Paul Cartledge, *Democracy: A Life*, 2nd edn (Oxford University Press 2018), p. 87.

14 Fuller, 'Enclosing the democratic commons', pp. 320 et seq.

15 Guy Standing, 'The precariat: why it needs more deliberative democracy', *Open Democracy* (27 January 2012), https://www.opendemocracy.net/guy-standing/ precariat-why-it-needs-deliberative-democracy (albeit in this version receipt of UBI should only entail a 'moral commitment' to vote).

16 Damien Tambini, '2018 will be the year in which liberal democracies begin to confront misinformation', *LSE Media Policy Project*, http://blogs.lse.ac.uk/mediapolicy project/2018/01/05/2018-beginning-of-the-end-for-fa ke-news/.

17 Owen Gibson, 'What the Sun said 15 years ago', *Guardian* (7 July 2004), https://www.theguardian.com/ media/2004/jul/07/pressandpublishing.football1.

18 'Full transcript of Gilligan's "sexed up" broadcast', *Guardian* (9 July 2003), https://www.theguardian.com/ media/2003/jul/09/Iraqandthemedia.bbc.

19 See, e.g., Tom Regan, 'When contemplating war, beware of babies in incubators', *Christian Science Monitor* (6 September 2002), https://www.csmonitor.com/2002/ 0906/p25s02-cogn.html; 'Deception on Capitol Hill', *New York Times Archive* (1992); Thomas E. Eidson, CEO Hills and Knowlton, Letter to the Editor, *New York Times* (15 January 1992).

20 Tambini, '2018 will be the year in which liberal democracies begin to confront misinformation'.

21 Dana Adams-Schmidt, 'Saudi Arabia: major changes due', *New York Times* (8 November 1964).

22 Paul L. Montgomery, 'Faisal, rich and powerful, led Saudis into 20th century', *New York Times* (26 March 1975).

23 Juan de Onis, 'Saudi king names his new cabinet', *New York Times* (30 March 1975).

24 Peter Kihss 'Man in the news; Saudi's king: ally of West: Fahd', *New York Times* (16 June 1982).

25 30 November 2013.

26 Aristotle, *The Athenian Constitution* (Sir Frederic G. Kenyon trans), XXII 4–7, http://classics.mit.edu/Aristotle/athenian_const.1.1.html.

27 Plutarch, 'Themistocles', *Parallel Lives*, 5.

28 Thucydides, *Peloponnesian War*, 1.5.

29 Plutarch, *Lives*.

30 Plutarch, *Lives*.

31 David Van Reybrouck, *Against Elections: The Case for Democracy* (Vintage 2016), p. 141.

32 Richard Wike, Katie Simmons, Bruce Stokes & Janell Fetterolf, 'Globally, broad support for representative and direct democracy', Pew Research Center (16 October 2017), http://www.pewglobal.org/2017/10/16/globally-broad-support-for-representative-and-direct-democracy/#fn-39248-1.

33 Christopher H. Achen & Larry M. Bartels, *Democracy for Realists: Why Elections Do Not Produce Responsive Government* (Princeton University Press 2016).

34 Ilya Somin, *Democracy and Political Ignorance: Why Smaller Government is Better*, 2nd edn (Stanford University Press 2016), pp. 106, 98 et seq.; Achen & Bartels, *Democracy for Realists*, pp. 30 et seq.

35 Achen & Bartels, *Democracy for Realists*, p. 33 (quoting Donald R. Kinder and Nathan Kalmoe, 'Neither liberal nor conservative: ideological innocence in the American electorate', unpublished manuscript); Ackerman & Fishkin, *Deliberation Day*, p. 129.

36 Achen and Bartels, *Democracy for Realists*, p. 294.

37 Sean Illing 'Two eminent political scientists: The problem with democracy is voters', *Vox* (24 June 2017), https://www.vox.com/policy-and-politics/2017/6/1/15515820/donald-trump-democracy-brexit-2016-election-europe.

38 Cass R. Sunstein, *#Republic: Divided Democracy in the Age of Social Media* (Princeton University Press 2017), is a title that frequently surfaces here.
39 Sasha Issenberg, 'How Obama's team used big data to rally voters', *MIT Technology Review* (19 December 2012), https://www.technologyreview.com/s/509026/how-obamas-team-used-big-data-to-rally-voters/.

Index

Achen, Christopher and Bartels, Larry
  identitarian politics, 14–15
  participation, 68
  political trivia, 36
  referenda, 45, 49
  in relation to other authors, 90–1
  shark attacks, 4, 55–64, 66–7
  short-cycle politics, 210
Askwith, Richard, 4, 112, 116, 137
Athenian assembly
  citizen participation, 113–14, 122, 158–9, 189–91
  functions and operations, 107–8, 110, 131, 173, 203
  pay, 165
  rationality, 129

basic social income (*see* universal basic income)
Bell, Daniel, 5, 90, 94–100, 102, 139
boule, 107–8, 113–14, 203

Brennan, Jason
  citizen participation, 5, 54, 69, 75–80
  in relation to other authors, 39, 80, 83, 87–8, 94, 99, 106
Brexit
  as racism, 13, 22–6
  in relation to majority rule, 2–4, 6, 30, 69, 72
  in relation to participatory democracy, 149, 154, 207–8
  in relation to sortition, 106, 112, 114, 123–6
  targeted ads, 214

Caplan, Bryan
  deep state, 80–3, 199
  enlightened preferences, 43–5
  rational ignorance, 30, 39–43
  in relation to other authors, 5, 83, 87–8, 94, 102, 106, 137, 139
China, 8, 94–9

Index

citizens' assemblies, 112, 119, 123–7, 135, 204
Clinton, Hillary, 13–18, 62–4, 70, 91
corruption
  in Athenian democracy, 130–1
  in China and Singapore, 95–8
  in mass participatory democracy, 147, 157, 198, 202–4
  in sortition, 130–7
  in Western democracies, 45, 48, 82, 89, 102, 143, 198, 202–4
Council of Five Hundred (*see boule*)

deliberation
  anti-democrat views, 69
  in relation to digital democracy, 148, 152, 158, 185–6, 188, 195–6, 205
  in relation to social media, 172, 177, 179, 184
  in relation to sortition, 127
digital democracy, 160, 167, 169, 204, 218

elections
  British, 5, 22, 26
  general, 101, 141, 144, 148
  Italian, 154
  Nicaragua, 81
  in relation to digital democracy, 167, 191, 197, 203, 211–12, 214
  in relation to sortition, 125, 128, 131–2, 134
  in relation to voter irrationality, 4, 37–8, 56–8, 61–7, 69

Switzerland, 25, 27
US presidential (2016), 2, 13, 17, 19, 24, 92
various American elections, 86, 89
electoral college, 62, 64
epistocracy, 5
Ethelo, 148–52

Farage, Nigel, 20–1, 194
FISA court, 92–3
Five-Star-Movement, 154
foot voting, 83–6, 105

Gore, Al, 61–4

Hopkins, Katie, 21–3

isegoria, 172–4, 177, 184–5

jury courts (Athens), 113, 191

local government, 201–2
lottery (*see* sortition)

mass participation
  Athens, 131, 136
  modern democracy, 140, 147–8, 154, 157–8, 170, 172, 199, 202–4
  sortition, 122, 136
mass participatory democracy, 140, 158, 196, 198, 203, 220
meritocracy, 5, 98, 100, 102

nomoi/nomos, 108, 110
nomothetai, 108, 110, 114

oligarchs/oligarchy, 143–4, 147, 168, 171, 204, 216

Index

online participatory platforms, 154

parrhesia, 173, 185
participatory budgeting, 35, 155–8, 202
partisan voting, 211
pay-for-participation, 165–6, 168–71, 196
people power, 137, 143, 147, 193, 220
Pirate Party, 154
PolCo, 152–3
policy jury, 112–13, 118, 128
Proposition 13, 46, 49, 51–3
psephisma/psephismata, 108–10

rational ignorance, 37, 76
Rauch, Jonathan, 137
  with Benjamin Wittes, 4, 69, 87–93, 95, 97, 102, 139
referenda
  Athens, 110
  Britain (*see* Brexit)
  California (*see* Proposition 13)
  in general, 26–7, 73
  Illinois, 46–9
  Ireland, 125–6, 204
  Quebec, 124
  Switzerland, 27
retrospective voting, 54, 64
rhetors, 189–90, 192–3, 195, 201, 204, 213, 218

Sanders, Bernie, 14–17, 91
sexism, 2, 12–16, 18, 20, 24–8, 68
slaves/slavery
  ancient, 159, 161–4, 165, 220
  modern, 25, 85
social media, 148, 154, 172, 177, 184–5
Somin, Ilya, 5, 39, 69, 83–8, 211
sortition
  executive, 196–205
  in juxtaposition to participatory democracy, 147, 165–6, 194–5
  legislative, 102–39

Themistocles, 192–194
Think-Long Committee, 100–2
troll/trolling, 179, 182–4
Trump, Donald, 2, 6, 13, 17–20, 24–7, 69, 81, 194, 214
trivia, 28, 30–1, 33–4, 36

UKIP, 3, 20, 22–3
universal basic income, 171, 188

van Reybrouck, David, 3–4, 112, 116, 127–8, 137, 208
virtue/virtuousness, 12, 82, 90, 94–9, 144

Wilson, Woodrow, 57–60, 62, 64, 67